The Form of Faith

The Form of Faith

Reflections on My Life, Romanticism, Meaning, and the Christian Faith in the Early 21st Century

James Prothero

RESOURCE *Publications* • Eugene, Oregon

THE FORM OF FAITH
Reflections on My Life, Romanticism, Meaning, and
the Christian Faith in the Early 21st Century

Resource Publications
An Imprint of Wipf and Stock Publishers
199 W. 8th Ave., Suite 3
Eugene, OR 97401

www.wipfandstock.com

PAPERBACK ISBN: 978-1-5326-1853-6
HARDCOVER ISBN: 978-1-4982-4418-3
EBOOK ISBN: 978-1-4982-4417-6

Manufactured in the U.S.A.

To Rev Dr Bruce W. Thielemann
of beloved memory
and
Dr Paul Ford
friend and guide

Preface

This work is something of a spiritual autobiography and something of an essay. That alone will expose it to criticism, as it is somewhat a hybrid. But I stand in a long and honorable line that way, going back to Lewis, Newman, and ultimately Augustine. Indeed, I have found thoughtful autobiography to shed far more light than abstract argumentation or pure unreflective autobiography. Moreover, this work was created in response to the question that loomed so large in my mind and with which I still wrestle: how does one live a Christian witness in the 21st century that is not culturally hijacked by political identification and can speak to the Millennial generation?

Is Christianity just a faded European cultural relic deserving its oncoming death? Has postmodernism negated all past traditions? Is there no longer any sense of right and wrong and are our moorings all cut loose? As a young man in the 1970s and 1980s, I dealt with these questions. I came to find C.S. Lewis to be a very useful guide. But even in admitting this, I immediately alienate those readers who resist the claims of Evangelical Christianity, and who assume (wrongly) that Lewis was the champion of an irrational American Fundamentalism. I found him to be anything but that. Yet the voices that guided me go far beyond Lewis. I am always brought back to the opening lines of Charles Dickens' novel *David Copperfield* in the first chapter titled: "I am born." The first sentence, which has ever haunted me, runs: "Whether I shall turn out to be the hero of my own life, or whether that station will be held by anybody else, these pages must show." It seems to me that for any person to be the hero of her or his own life, they must make the pilgrimage to a knowledge that grants him or her peace. I do not argue for Christianity in the sense that I must convert all the world. First, Christ himself said that this was not possible (Matt 7:14) and the whole mentality smacks of a kind of imperialism that longs for a consistent theological rule over a large population. Some people even today—Christians, or so they claim—talk of this as if it were desirable to have a Christian theocracy and universal Christian professed belief of the kind that was in Europe through the Middle Ages. The last time it was tried, it led to vast corruption in the Church and was more effective in creating an imperial monarchy that ruled all of Europe than on bringing Christ to humanity. The Reformation pretty much put an end to that. Many Protestants talk as if being Protestant rendered them immune to the same error, as if they were free of the temptation to go from theocracy to tyranny, a fact which makes me shudder.

Second, as Chesterton observed, Christianity dies from time to time and is then mysteriously resurrected. I suspect that here in the first quarter of the 21st century, we are seeing a die-off. In my country, sadly, most people associate the word "Christianity" with political conservatism, so that for many, Christianity is fast becoming merely a synonym for the far right, and the claims of Christ merely a smoke screen for dragooning one into far-right politics. This alliance between Evangelical and conservative, which many think is moral and right, is here in 2016 driving the younger generation away in droves.

The second mark of death, at least in the American church, is the refusal to recognize scientific reality. My father was a technical illustrator and worked for Lockheed Aircraft for most of the Cold War. He was surrounded by technology on a daily basis, and furthermore had a deep respect for what could honestly be discovered using the scientific method of inquiry and impeccable honesty. For many years he could not bring himself to go to church because of the people there who willfully misunderstood the issues in the controversy over Evolution. He did not live to see it, but he would have shaken his head over those who deny climate change and thought in terms of large *ad hominum* fallacies, such as that all scientists were crazy, lying liberals and therefore not to be believed.

This may sell in the Tea Party, but the upcoming generation finds it absurd the way my father did, so they turn away.

But then there's the other side of the equation. Some elements of the church in America that characterize themselves as "liberal" are prone to believe nothing and everything. If they go as far as Universalism, it really doesn't matter what one believes. The belief in the first century Jewish carpenter is mixed liberally with one's own ideas and anything that appeals to one. Why anyone would want to become such a Christian is to me beyond explanation. Most such people have been raised in one strict denomination and moved to a more vague and pleasant set of beliefs, perhaps if nothing else, in order to find comfort.

Where is there a Christianity that might actually draw people to Christ? And why in this diverse world and nation should we want such a Christianity? How did I find such a Christianity? These are the questions I wish to explore. I cannot hand out indisputable universal maxims. What I can do is tell my story.

One: Sunday School Jesus

> The Child is the father of the Man;
> And I could wish my days to be
> Bound each to each by natural piety.
>
> —FROM THE "IMMORTALITY ODE" WILLIAM WORDSWORTH

I was born in the mid-fifties in a conservative white suburb north of Los Angeles known as Glendale. It was a truly Ozzie and Harriet world except for two atypical things that would shape me. My father was a short man with a "butch" haircut and glasses, quiet, kind, though with the capacity for a formidable anger when he smelt injustice or petulant disobedience. My mother was the classic pretty 50s wife and homemaker, who had been raised Presbyterian. My Dutch-American grandmother had promised a priest to raise my mother and her siblings as Catholics, when she married my Irish-American grandfather. But grandmother was a staunch Protestant at heart, and couldn't bring herself to keep that promise. So my mother grew up in the Glendale Presbyterian Church, a huge, red-brick edifice in downtown Glendale, that somewhat resembled a cross between a cathedral and a castle. My first experience of Christianity as a small boy was that it was impressive, something that went on in massive buildings to pipe organ music of the kind that accompanied the creation of the universe.

From the first moment, I found myself in the presence of my elder brother, Donald. Of Donald, much can be said. He has since made a considerable reputation in the worlds of paleontology and natural science. But probably my first awareness was of this other boy in the children's room that seemed to have always been there. He was a mere year and a half older, so we were effectively like twins. But we were not at all alike: whereas Don was and is a scientist, I am a Romantic (but more on that later). Don was and is, bloody brilliant, as the British would say. And he always had a sense of his gift, which, I believe, drove him to be competitive. At age four he loudly announced that he would be a "dinosaur scientist", a resolve which he never wavered from. His fascination was science, and specifically the question of where everything came from and what was here before, beyond the known precincts of history.

I bring all this up because one of the first charges against Christian faith is that it is merely a cultural relic that Europeans and Euro-Americans slip into because they don't know any better. But I can't believe this; my experience is different. Don was taken to Sunday School where some teacher, a middle-class, white businessman with little education outside college, where he majored, no doubt, in business and thought of little else, tried to sell Don the Fundamentalist view of the first chapters of Genesis. Don, probably around seven at the time, argued passionately that the man hadn't read his science, which was doubtlessly true. I don't know what the man did. My guess is that he probably didn't sign up for teaching Sunday School again. But for Don this was a supreme moment of self-definition. He slipped into no form of cultural Christianity. Instead he bucked. Sometime in high school, he and my mother came to an understanding, and except for weddings and funerals, he never attended church again. There was no pressure, no push from my parents to explain that all decent people are Christian, nor similar arguments. They believed no such thing. They felt no such cultural pressure, which was part of the reason why my Dad did not attend church. Don was allowed to believe what he believed. And this is the legacy of my parents that wasn't quite so Ozzie and Harriet. I may have been exposed to the Evangelical Protestant world view, but the very air I breathed at home was the air of intellect and creativity.

My father, though he was by profession a technical artist, was a man of science; more precisely, he had the soul of an engineer. He had been raised in the faith, but he firmly believed that God was never threatened by the truth, and if there was a conflict between perceivable truth and what Christian teachers taught, those teachers had got it wrong. This fact for years kept him out of the Evangelical Presbyterian churches my mother preferred. Holding this inviolable dedication to truth may seem a very simple principle, but you can already see how this must have influenced my brother on that Sunday morning of his battle with the teacher. And it influenced all of us. It was a pole around which our world spun. Nor have I ever felt the slightest shame nor regret about having such a position in my own mind.

The second pole would be that though my mother was an Evangelical, and attended women's Bible study almost every week of her adult life until dementia began to take her mind, she was also an artist. The visual arts were part of my growing up. There was never a time in my home when there wasn't a room designated as an art studio. My father was a supervisor in the art and printing department of Lockheed Aircraft. By the time I reached college age, he was the manager of the department. He met my mother in 1950 or 1951 because she had some art training and was working there. In fact, she defied company policy and married her boss in 1952. Our house was always full of books and art and I grew up in that rich environment. My own tastes run to the impressionists and post-impressionists, but my parents were eclectic. I recall several abstract paintings hanging around the house, one of which was a print of a Wassily Kandinsky painting.

So as a Christian in America, I have often felt out of step with Evangelicals who believe that scientists lie and that art is immoral. I was raised to be anything but anti-intellectual and puritanical and I have never had much patience nor pity for either tendency. I was raised in a world where there was no conflict between science and Christ, science and truth, nor Christ and truth. And it was also a world where beauty and creativity were to be pursued, not to be ashamed of or limited to some form that inevitably had to do with hard-sell evangelism. Art was there because God, the Ultimate Artist, created it, and it was to be celebrated. And science was the act of discovery of all the things in nature that God has done. Neither were anything to be ashamed of or somehow limited in order to accommodate someone's narrow reading of scripture.

Around the time I was five, my Dad was transferred to Sunnyvale, California, for almost two years. There my younger brother, John, was born. I have always gravitated to the visual arts like my father, but also inherited his love of literature. Indeed, all of us brothers have devoted our lives to one or more of my father's wide interests. Donald embraced my Dad's interest in science. John grew to become the photographer that most followed in my Dad's footsteps with a camera. John also was the artist, but with his voice and has since sung with professional grade choral groups. Although my Dad was never a singer, his love of all the arts, and the world of art he created around us brothers as we grew up, made this possible for John. But the Sunnyvale adventure did not last long. My dad was transferred back to Lockheed Burbank and we returned to Glendale with baby John to a house in an area known as the Verdugo Woodlands.

So this was my world where from an early age, I became well-acquainted with the stories and the content of the Bible through my mother and through my church. Fortunately for me, I never had the Sunday School teacher tell me that the earth was created in six days, something that would have made me uncomfortable. Like Don, I would have felt the need to correct the teacher, but however I lacked Don's confidence to speak up. I got to know first the Sunday School Jesus. He was white, and had kindly eyes with a slight smile in all the art I saw. I have always been visual, so this was vital to my perceptions from the beginning. Also what was interesting from the beginning is that I felt a distrust for the images from the start. I lived a life fairly insulated from black, brown and red America, but I instinctively felt they were out there. So how did I begin to suspect that the safe, white, Evangelical, middle class world wasn't everything? Perhaps it was the genial children's television host, Captain Kangaroo, who did much to educate my young mind, (and to whom I am eternally grateful) who made a point of showing videos made of picture books that featured children of many races. And being the reader I was with access to Bibles—there were probably fifteen of them laying around the house at any given time—I read not only the passages where Christ was loving and reassuring, but the passages where he was severe, of which we heard less at Sunday School. And though I was too young to express it, I sensed even then that there was more than the world I saw and knew, and more than just the sweet and friendly Sunday School Jesus. Perhaps it was little hints in Sunday School songs like, "Red and yellow, black and white/ They are precious in His sight/ Jesus loves the little children of the world." And why should this Jesus, who lived in the Middle East, look white? After all, wouldn't Jesus look more like an Arab? My father's endless supply of *National Geographics* had given me a visual clue what Middle Eastern people looked like. I wondered.

One thing Captain Kangaroo accomplished with me was to make me a researcher long before I knew what that was. I recall as a young boy discussing my "favorite subject" with my friends. I found myself surprised that I was one of the few that had a subject upon which I was reading everything I could get my hands on, and that this subject changed from time to time and that I considered that normal behavior. My parents surrounded me with books, but the Captain gave me my love of literacy, and the love of the intellectual and literary pleasures of exploring the world on the pages of a book. Of course, my parents knew what they were doing and were happy to park me in front of the television if the Captain was on. They did not allow me to watch just anything, but the Captain was a recognized blessing and I ate it up with my brothers, who were likewise bookish and born researchers. If there were any conflicts with my parents over television it was my love of Warner Brothers cartoons, Jay Ward cartoons and Tom and Jerry. But my folks needn't have worried. From the wise creators of Bugs Bunny, Rocky and Bullwinkle, and Tom and Jerry, I learned irony and just how odd the world is, and how laughter is pretty much the only thing one can sanely do with what life hands us. It gave me my love of irony which my students since have often remarked on.

So the ink line and watercolor Jesus of the Sunday School materials was the first thing I experienced in Christianity. The one other thing was that my mother rose early every morning and read her Bible and said prayers in the holy stillness of first light. I still do so to this day.

Two: Summer Camp and Finding Another World

Small service is true service while it lasts;
Of Friends, however humble, scorn not one:

—"Yarrow Revisited", William Wordsworth

There were many other events in my young life that I would include if this were a pure autobiography. I had a few startling and generational memories, my own private Forest Gump history. For example, I was a live witness to the shooting of Lee Harvey Oswald. My parents managed to shield us boys from the coverage of the murder of President Kennedy, but they slipped up with me on Oswald. I happened to be at home from second grade, sick with a cold and watching TV movies with my mother on the morning of November 24, 1963. As she stepped out of the room to hang some shirts she'd ironed, the news flash interrupted the movie, and I saw the whole murder live. When she returned to the room, the confused TV station crew had returned to the movie. I told my mother what I'd seen and she didn't believe me until the broadcast was taken over by the news department soon thereafter.

But the central feature of my boyhood years is that I had a wonderful friendship with a boy whose parents were English, and who shared my imagination and love of research, though we wouldn't have recognized it as such. He was Nigel Taylor, and we had all sorts of "favorite subjects", including an obscure band from Britain called The Beatles. His British cousins sent him all the first release vinyl and we took badminton rackets and played air guitar to their music. With Nigel's partnership and encouragement, my interests ranged far and I read copiously. This probably made up for the fact that I was diagnosed with some form of ADD and was almost unable to concentrate in school—that and the fact that my baseball-player grandfather had passed zero genes of athletic ability down to me. So I was a frustration to my teachers and I was broke in the currency that schoolchildren judge each other by: skill at games. I could please nobody. Teachers knew I was smart, but unless the lesson engaged my imagination, my mind wandered elsewhere. This was the era of learning math by drill-and-kill and I don't doubt that the endless rows of arithmetic problems repeated for no discernible reason killed whatever interest I ever had in math, closing the door to the sciences for me beyond a layman's fascination. I lived in two worlds: the rich imaginative world that books, and my father's vast breadth of knowledge afforded me at home, versus the world where I was the clumsy, skinny, quiet kid who was no good at games and didn't do much school work. Ironically, as a future teacher, elementary school was a torment to me.

But I did have a defining moment in faith. It was either the summer of my third or fourth grade year, making it either the summer of 1965 or 1966. My parents sent me to church camp in the mountains. It was called "Indian Village" and it was in the Mill Creek Valley of the eastern San Bernardino Mountains, part of a complex of camps connected to Billy Graham's organization, called "Forest Home." One of my fascinations was Native Americans, so I was very up for this. We lived in canvas tepees and there were ceremonies that pretended to be Indian. I had a blast. Years later, when I knew more, I realized that the "Indian Village" version of Native American life owed everything to the Hollywood version and nothing to any genuine research. But that did not affect me at the time.

One afternoon, our counselor, who was probably no more than eighteen himself and very halting and unsure in his speech, assembled us all in our tepee and gave us the classical Evangelical spiel about accepting Jesus Christ as our personal savior. Jesus was no stranger to my home; my mother spent every morning with him and sang us songs about him to put us to sleep at night. I did sort of feel like a fish being informed about the existence of water. Yet, somewhere in this teenaged boy's halting, awkward language there were words about committing your life to Christ. I may have been young, but I did understand I was being asked to sign over the papers on my soul. What could a child understand, you might ask. Well, I could understand quite a lot at that age, probably due to my father's answering every question we ever fired at him from his vast general knowledge. Though my brother Don was not there, I am sure at some point he had the same experience and assuredly did *not* sign on the dotted line. He knew what he was doing then, and he has stayed with that conviction all these years. But I knew what I was doing too. I said yes.

Now, my theology is such that I don't place much weight on altar calls and showy, emotional one-time conversion experiences. Conversion is a long, long process and I've always had a problem with the Evangelical idea that we can get people to say they accept Jesus and then just move on and leave them in the dust. That is theologically irresponsible if not comically naive. Furthermore, it seems odd to call this a conversion experience since I arrived at camp believing Jesus was the Son of God and left the same way. What was different was that I knew I was signing over the pink slip of my soul and I made the conscious choice to do it. If I were going to characterize it now I would say that I chose to pass on merely being a "cultural Christian", to just play the game of faith halfheartedly and for show. I signed on for the full treatment without anyone there to push me either way. I, who could barely swim, dove head first into the sea of faith.

The counselor was far too awkward to ask any of us to speak up. If we made the decision he asked us to, we kept it to ourselves. Indeed, looking back, I wonder if he fully believed it himself, or if this awkward talk he had to give was the price he had to pay for the small salary and the chance to hang out in the mountains for free. I don't remember his name and little more than his face. I don't know what happened to him. But though I'm sure he never knew, he set an earthquake going in my life.

I was aware, even in those years after my tepee commitment, of trying to live the life Christ talks about in the Sermon on the Mount. But how does a little boy do that when he's the school pariah for his total lack of athletic skill, and far from being the teacher's pet for his lack of ability to concentrate on and complete mundane tasks? Let's just say I had a lot of practice in forgiveness. I lived in those two worlds, the disappointing world of the school where I was inadequate to everyone, and the second world of books and ideas and knowledge, which was exhilarating. And then my wonderful second world opened out when my father took Don and me, and my grandmother east of the Colorado River to the magical land of Arizona and the Four Corners states. I can't recall if we were in a car or a camper. I think it was a car, but that detail is unimportant. We saw Zion and Kayenta I know—and I believe we visited the site of my grandparents' former ranch in southwest Colorado. I don't recall much else. Yet, it was for me as rich and magical as reaching Narnia. And I have been in love with that country ever since.

But something far more significant happened on that trip, something that had been brewing in my soul for some time: I discovered that I was a Romantic. I do not use this word carelessly. I have since earned a PhD in British Romanticism; I am a Wordsworth scholar. So I mean something very precisely when I say that the first trip to Arizona and the Four Corners, (and all subsequent trips as well,) confirmed in me a Romanticism that I was probably born with. I mean that I experienced what Wordsworth experienced at the top of Mt. Snowdon or when he toured the Wye Valley around Tintern Abbey—I experienced those surging feelings and thoughts witnessing the painted desert of Navajoland and the high forests of northern Arizona, southeast Utah, southwestern Colorado, and New Mexico. I experienced Keats' and Coleridge's sublime. This is vital, for how can one talk about faith without talking about this quintessentially religious experience? People have often accused Romanticism of being a substitute for faith. But I have never accepted that idea. I rather suspect that Romanticism is one of the more common doors into faith, without which, many of us would have been incapable of believing in, nor beginning to comprehend the glory of God.

So picture me: I was perhaps ten or eleven years old, a gawky, skinny boy, with thick glasses and high water pants, socially inept, unathletic, and a bane to my teachers. And I was a soaring Romantic, feeling what Wordsworth felt, standing on the holy land of the Dine People, Dinetah, my heart leaping up at the sight of the San Juan Mountains of Colorado, as Wordsworth's heart leaped up standing on the top of Mt. Snowdon, looking over the moonlit sea of fog. I'm not sure whether such an image is more inspirational or absurdly comic. I suspect the latter.

Three: Joy and Junior High

> He [Nicholas] could not but observe how silent and sad the boys all seemed to be. There was none of the noise and clamour of a schoolroom; none of its boisterous play, or hearty mirth. The children sat crouching and shivering together, and seemed to lack the spirit to move about .
>
> —*Nicholas Nickleby* by Charles Dickens

Now that I've brought up Romanticism, I am remiss if I don't mention another important element. Call it "joy." The Romantics named it many things, but I knew this inexplicable and unpredictable euphoria that would come with beauty in some form, like happiness, but far richer and stronger, that left one wondering if anything else in life was worth experiencing after that magnificent surge. It is clearly a part of my Romanticism, but I strongly suspect that everyone experiences it in some form. I also suspect that most people live mainly to experience it, though they couldn't tell you that in a few words. For me, as for others, it came through art and stories, and sunrises and the beauty of nature. Our frequent trips across the Colorado River were often done in early morning, so I came to associate being on a highway at sunrise with joy. I still find this experience of sunrise roads to be one of the most satisfying experiences I have ever had. This joy was part of my second world that included books and ideas and art and travel.

The first world shifted on me rather suddenly. I found myself in what we called then, junior high, though it's now known as middle school. My parents, in despair of my ADD refusal to work in school, had placed me in a private school, a strategy that had no effect. If, Romantic that I was and am, the assignment did not engage my imagination, I zoned out and didn't do it. When the school I'd been attending, Salem Lutheran, ended with sixth grade, I was put in another school for seventh grade, that was part of a conservative Missouri Synod church. I had learned much more about the Sunday School Jesus in my first Lutheran elementary school, as well as Martin Luther and just how wonderful *he* was. The two were rather a package in the books they gave us. And Luther was clearly up there with the Apostle Paul. Even at that age I was able to discern the partisan difference between this and the view of Luther in my Presbyterian Church, and thus suspect that there were different schools of thought. Where did I stand? The question was raised but not answered for some time.

However, this new Lutheran junior high school, compared to the other, was a prison. It evokes for me even now, all the horror that Dickens, and later Lewis portrayed in literature of the tyrannical school. We were regimented to the point that we were never let out of sight of the teacher, whom I will call "Mr. M", not even for lunch. Education was a fierce forced march through curriculum with Mr. M threatening dire consequences at all times. This was going on at the height of the hippie movement, and I think these conservative Lutherans felt it was their duty to whack some discipline back into a young generation going astray. I went from the Sunday School Jesus to the stern, frowning, puritanical, pharisaical Jesus. I was not disillusioned about what had happened to my faith; I knew Mr. M and these people were wrong and perhaps a bit mad from one defining moment which came early in the year of my sentence. But I was the quiet kid who survived by keeping my head down.

The defining moment was when we were singing the morning hymn. I normally liked singing and the hymn was a simplification of the final movement of Beethoven's ninth symphony to joy, a melody I still love. For some reason I don't recall, I was sad that morning and let the others sing. Mr. M looked at my mouth, walked up to me and ordered me to sing for joy, "or else!" I complied, but in that moment I understood the nature of the theology and faith of that brand of Christianity. Compliance and conformity *were* holiness in that creed. I find this ironic in hindsight, because as good conservative Lutherans, they would have been quick to criticize the Catholic Church for Pelagianism, that is, for mistaking human action for grace. Yet, this is exactly what they did themselves; they defined holiness and being "saved" by how conservative you are dressed, how often you showed up for Sunday worship, and whether you used the correct Church English. They were flagrant Pelagians opposed to Pelagianism and they didn't know it. I didn't know what it was about their version of Christianity at that time, but I was sure even at thirteen years old, that this theology had little to nothing to do with the Jesus I read about in the Bible, that I had signed on with in that tepee. And finally, though I was smart enough to not laugh at Mr. M to his face, I was perceptive enough to think the stern order to sing for joy to be supremely and hilariously funny. As I said, Bugs, Rocky, and Bullwinkle had taught me the irony of absurdity. But I didn't yet have a friend to share it with till I left that school.

I recall that the only light in that joyless cave was a Chicano classmate named Felix, who was probably put there for the discipline. But Felix was no real rebel or cholo. Felix was simply one of those irrepressible people who are delighted with life as it comes to them and act on impulse. For them, they can no more stop from laughing and finding the fun in things than they can stop breathing. There was no harm in Felix, no cruelty, and much real mirth. One of the tyrannies was that Mr. M would have us eat lunch in silence under his glare, while he played the absurd broadcasts of Paul Harvey on his radio. To this day I cannot bear to listen to replays of Paul Harvey—in the past whenever anyone insisted on turning him in, I left the room. But nature was on our side, and every once in a while, Mr. M too had to go and relieve himself. Felix would pop up the minute Mr. M was gone and change the station to the most popular pop/rock station at the time, KHJ radio. When Mr. M came back, he would be furious and demand to know the culprit who had let in the evil and anti-Christian rock 'n roll, as he turned the dial back to Paul Harvey. We may have been obsequious slaves to the tyrant but we had enough collective spine not to give up Felix to punishment. Mr. M never figured it out, though I think he suspected correctly it must have been Felix. My best teacher that year was Felix—I learned much from him about courage in the face of tyranny and the ability to laugh when all the world seems dark.

I say Felix was my best teacher, but Mr. M taught me that year far more than curriculum. From him I first experienced the Conservative Narrative. I came to know it far better later in life, but even at this point already I could see it with something of an objective distance. I said above that I recognized Mr. M's Christianity to be a little mad. Let me explain that in depth.

I won't claim that I understood everything I'm about to say now, when I was in junior high. I still had a long road ahead of me at this point in my life. But this was my first experience with the Conservative Narrative, and though I was pretty ignorant, it tasted wrong to me. Perhaps this was because I knew my parents didn't think that way. Whatever the reason, as I learned more over the decades, I never came to repent my initial distaste for it.

I call it a narrative because it was and is basically a story. Years later, when I was a college professor teaching critical thinking at Orange Coast College, I found it to be pointless to just teach deductive thinking in a mathematical way when what students really wrestled with were the arguments that swirled around their lives on a daily basis. And most of these arguments were ultimately political. I taught them that our thinking is not purely deductive. If anyone doesn't know or recall deductive, it is what I call chain logic. I know A and B, therefore I can deduce that C is true, and so on. Every conclusion lies at the end of a series of facts. I told my students that it would be lovely if we all could live by pure logic like Mr. Spock from *Star Trek*, but that life on Earth was messier than it was on planet Vulcan. I taught them that all of us start our thinking from basic assumptions. And I defined assumption as something that you believed to be true but that you could neither prove nor disprove. When Jefferson wrote "We hold these truths to be self-evident" he was talking about what I called assumptions. In the case of vast political and philosophical positions like conservative and liberal, these assumptions are so far developed that they form a myth and a story. I have to be careful with the word "myth." Most people today think it means the same as a lie. I am using a portion of Lewis' definition of it. He tells us that "The experience [of myth] is not only grave but awe-inspiring. We feel it to be numinous. It is as if something of great moment had been communicated to us." These are stories in which even the recitation of their mere plot hold transcendent and archetypal resonances.[1]

Thus Romeo and Juliet is myth, far beyond just the Shakespeare play or the Italian story he took it from. It is the eternal and quintessential story of the hopelessness and yet beauty of romantic love, and the fact that it often ends in tragedy. The story helps us understand what love means in all its beauty and pain. And this is what myth does for us: it explains meaning through a story.

What I first began to get from Mr. M and from Paul Harvey on the radio I would call the Conservative Myth as well as the Conservative Narrative. Paul Harvey was the Rush Limbaugh of his day, though he didn't specialize in righteous rage like Rush. His style was dripping irony with long pauses that made me wish the radio had stopped working and that he'd blessedly fallen silent. No such luck.

I would go one step beyond Lewis and define a myth as a story from which people derive essential meaning. A myth tells you who you are and what life means. And it generally comes in the form of a story, a narrative. The conservative narrative is pretty well known and runs roughly as follows: Individualism is not only our birthright, it is a principal tenet of Christianity. Private property is also a Christian right. Personal responsibility is important and "if a man will not work, let him not eat." But most of all, these liberties must be guarded from government, which is more likely to be the problem than the solution.

That is not the whole of the narrative. But it has the essential elements. To be fair, liberalism has its own myth and narrative,

1. Lewis, *Experiment in Criticism*, 44.

which I find almost equally incredible. Whereas conservatives raise individualism and individual rights to a religious principal, liberals do so with equality and tolerance. Community is also a higher value for liberals. My problem with both narratives is that there are elements of truth in each of them, but these truths are pushed out to some logical, or perhaps illogical extreme to the point that the person that holds them has to deny a certain degree of reality in order to maintain their pure and undiluted philosophy. Thus I think if we truly are Christian, we cannot put individualism over community to the degree that we let people suffer. The Good Samaritan did not cite his personal rights and move on past the wounded traveler. Yet, as Lewis deplored an all -powerful state, I would too. It's not a matter of who is right, and who is wrong. It's a matter of applying sometimes conflicting principals in a balanced way in a complex world. Pure philosophies sound good on paper; they don't deal well with reality.

In addition, some extremes on either side seemed to me obtuse. On the liberal side, tolerance pushed to the point where one denied the existence of truth was laughably preposterous. And confusing equality of access, something right and necessary, with equality of results was also a twisting of reality. People are all different. If you give everyone a fair start, they are not all going to finish the race at the same moment. And their failing to do so doesn't automatically mean the start was faulty. And I fear the possibility of the sense of community turning to a collectivist tyranny as much as any conservative. But that doesn't mean we throw out all community. What is needed is not a holy war from the left or the right; what is needed is balance.

On the conservative side, individualism was elevated to a place of higher importance than the teachings of Christ, and with some strained effort of interpretation, the differences between Christ's teachings and individualism were denied. Indeed, denial of emerging realities seemed to be the hallmark of the movement, whether they be science, faith, or that simple confronting of our own sinful racism. But beyond that, for me the single most obtuse thing about conservatism was Tim McVeigh Fallacy.

All this fear and hatred of the government I call Tim McVeigh Fallacy. McVeigh, as many will recall, built a bomb to blow up the hated government. He set it off next to a government building in Oklahoma City in 1995. And when the dust had cleared what we all found was that he had killed fathers, mothers, husbands, wives, sons, daughters, even little children. It is a fallacy to talk about government as one single, huge, evil, malicious entity. It isn't. Government is us. It's Americans, as McVeigh proved in such a lethal manner. When I hear someone complain that they don't want the government, what I hear is they don't want to be part of America, to share the burdens and difficulties of community. That's what taxes do. I hear them saying that they would rather live as a one-person nation to themselves off in the wild. Such attitudes show an ignorance of how much we all count on each other and on the infrastructure we build and provide for each other. It's a fallacy and a form of short-sightedness.

Conservatives deplore government, but what else is there if we are to work together as a nation on anything? Sure it can be bumbling and ineffective at times, but that's *us* being bumbling and ineffective, not some evil alien power. Some talk as if we could return to the frontier of the old West, where individualism and law out of a gun barrel were all that one needed. How is that possible in an increasingly urban and technological America? Even the Old Testament has God holding nations collectively responsible. How are we to be collectively responsible if we cannot work together and elect leadership because it might become a government?

These pure, pre-packaged philosophies, so popular now, always for me smelled suspect. Granted, my sense of community and my respect for science and the environment probably leads some to accuse me of being more left than right, but if that's so, it's because so much of the right seems to me to deny the complexity of reality and the fact that the world does change over time, whether you want it to or not.

As I said, in that moment Mr. M barked at me to sing for joy, I understood the nature of the theology and faith of that brand of Christianity increasingly merged with conservatism: compliance and conformity *were* holiness in that creed. Mr. M needed to make all of us do what was Correct. That was the meaning of being American and Christian. Looking back now I see how seductive that line of thought is. How comforting to be able to simply glance at someone or listen to them for five minutes and know whether or not they're a patriotic American and are going to Heaven. How convenient.

So Mr. M and Paul Harvey first introduced me to the conservative narrative. I gagged a little, especially on Paul Harvey. It wasn't till I met Bruce Thielemann that I began to see more. But that's another chapter.

Four: Blessed Liberty and Gregg

> A man's life of any worth is a continual allegory—and very few eyes can see the mystery of life—a life like the Scriptures, figurative . . . .
>
> —John Keats

My parents told me that if my grades went up, I could escape my prison and rejoin my brothers in public school. At this point, whatever effect the ADD had on me, I was outgrowing it somehow, and the possibility of escape from tyranny was enough to cause me to become a rather good student. My grades shot up like a balloon trapped under water and released. I do admit with some shame that it was not until I'd been in college for some time that I became as hard-working and good a student as I was really capable of. And I had a very poor reason for this. Donald by this time was an honor-roll student and fiercely competitive in academic circles. Perhaps it was Donald's influence, but I was as disinclined to be competitive as he was inclined to be competitive. Maybe I learned the best way to compete with Donald was not to compete. In that junior high and later high school atmosphere heavy with peer pressure, I did not want to be compared to Don. I was smart enough to get Bs without trying too hard, so that is what I did. And the habit unfortunately stayed with me all through undergraduate school.

In the eighth grade I was liberated and granted the right to go to public junior high. There I saw more beautiful young girls around me than I thought were possible in the world. One pretty girl named Rita, with long, black hair, who sat next to me in typing class, almost caused me to unravel on the floor. I was never one of those boys who disliked girls when I was in elementary. I never said, "Ew! Girls! Yuk!" or pretended to be disgusted by them. More likely I was to be found playing house with them when I was small, and casting admiring glances thereafter. There was always a girl I had a crush on. I always was in awe of women, of their beauty in all its various forms and of the goodness and grace they bestow on the human race. And I still am. I am an inveterate philogynist—a lover of women. This may seem a funny point to bring up, but I have often wondered if it was the boys who hated girls when those boys were still in elementary school who subsequently abused their wives, daughters, and girlfriends in adulthood. I remember having a crush on one young beauty in my class, Sharon Fitzgerald, which led me to do a rather good pastel portrait of her. I caught her in the hall one day and gave it to her. She was very gracious and started talking to me with interest, while I stood there mainly tongue-tied and stupid. Then she thanked me and walked away. I felt a mix of relief that she liked the portrait and frustration that I couldn't do more with the conversation but sweat and stutter.

I had some really good teachers at Wilson: Alma Cailor and Maryann Visokey laid the foundations of my knowledge in English, which became my profession. There was a brilliant and creative social studies teacher named Dennis Ericson whose insights I still recall and revere, and even a good math teacher named Gardner, a man dripping with hilarious, sardonic irony, who succeeded in making my worst subject palatable. But my favorite was Saul Cohen. He was my art teacher, a light but muscular man in his 30s with long, bushy black hair and a bushy black beard. He invariably preferred to wear collared shirts with the sleeves rolled up and jeans, a habit that I later adopted and never gave up, perhaps in admiration of him and his attitude towards life and art. I have had art teachers whom in the name of creativity have let their students do whatever appealed to them. It didn't often work. Cohen understood that really good art required a great deal of self-discipline. Every class we walked into, we were hard at work drawing and/or painting, and there was something to work on.

Either there was a still life set up for a few days, or just as often, Cohen would summon a student to model, and our class became a life drawing class. I think I learned more about drawing and painting from Cohen than all my other art teachers since. He died in a tragedy not long after I left the school, but he was an art teaching genius. God rest him.

If I was awkward before this, junior high was an awkwardness minefield—and I managed to step on pretty much every mine. Yet, there were two high points. Nigel had faded away from me, sadly. However, in junior high I met another British boy, Gregg Brown, who became my best friend. Together we slogged through the minefield of junior high. Gregg was brilliant in sciences and math, but we shared the love of imagination and found that we liked our company better than all the people around us who didn't share our interests. Those interests were far-ranging and infinite, from hiking, to books, to building projects and sometimes to just discussing life, faith and philosophy. Gregg was agnostic and didn't see the point of my church commitment. But he never criticized me for it, so we got along. And Gregg shared my lack of athletic prowess and my admiration from afar of all the beautiful women around us. His humor was a cross between Monty Python and Groucho Marx, and he taught me to fully love verbal irony, understatement, and absurdity as the preferred modes of humor. The banter that I keep up in a classroom today to keep students awake is stolen directly from Gregg, and I find it has been an effective teaching mode for over 30 years now.

As I seem to find defining moments everywhere, I'll try to find one for Gregg. But there are too many candidates. I will pick two: "insegrievious", and the giant paper airplane. Gregg one day heard a radio comedian use the word, "insegrievious." He was terribly intrigued. It sounded like it should really be a word that educated people should know. It had weight. One imagined some somber minister using it at a funeral or a CEO using it at a board meeting. But the real genius of insegrievious was that, beyond the fact it was some sort of adjective, it had no meaning whatsoever, and that was the beauty of it. Later on, as the radio comedian used it, it came to mean irritating and disgusting. But that only emerged later. We loved the word precisely because it sounded so meaningful and was entirely meaningless. One could just drop it in a conversation on some unsuspecting victim. "I was insegrievious about that political speech yesterday." Most people are too proud to admit that you know a word that they don't, so they might nod their heads and say, "I totally get what you're saying," when in fact, they hadn't the foggiest notion of what you're talking about.

The paper airplane though was a quintessential Gregg and I sort of thing to do. One day in a book I learned a different way of making paper airplanes that had some airfoil in the wings and weight in the nose. Thus it flew much better than traditional long, triangular airplanes. Gregg and I wondered what would happen if we made it bigger. We got a hold of a large sheet of construction paper and carefully reproduced the instructions meant for an 8.5x10 piece of paper. Gregg, physicist that he was, calculated the different flight characteristics that shape and size would cause. It was magnificent, with a wingspan of almost a yard. We took it up on a hillside in our neighborhood and let it go in a good tailwind. It soared for at least two minutes before crashing into someone's back yard where a dog was barking furiously. The change in the noise the dog was making told us the fate of our airship after it landed without us having to guess too hard. But the flight was so 'Gregg and I,' such an optimistic mixture of my romantic vision of a grand airplane coupled with his physics of making it precisely correct so that it would fly, watching it spin on the wind, and the final irony of it becoming dog food. I couldn't have written a better script for my adventures with Gregg.

Five: Bruce and Christ the Tiger

Our revels now are ended. These our actors,
As I foretold you, were all spirits and
Are melted into air, into thin air:
And, like the baseless fabric of this vision,
The cloud-capp'd towers, the gorgeous palaces,
The solemn temples, the great globe itself,
Yea, all which it inherit, shall dissolve
And, like this insubstantial pageant faded,
Leave not a rack behind. We are such stuff
As dreams are made on, and our little life
Is rounded with a sleep.

—*The Tempest*, Act 4, Scene 1, William Shakespeare

My real revolution and second high point on the spiritual side of things was that during this era my church called a minister by the name of Bruce W. Thielemann. Bruce was a large, overweight man with very little hair and a look on his face that I suppose Napoleon had as he led his armies to battle. And battle was Bruce's primary mode. He wasn't always popular with his church staff, nor the elements in the congregation who were conservative and liked to be told on Sunday mornings that their prosperity and church-going made them good Christians. Bruce had a bit of the bull in the china shop in him, and he liked to discomfit the comfortable. Tact was optional and intelligent assertion mandatory. What Bruce was really good at was sermons. He was perhaps one of the finest orators in America in the late 20th century. Already, with his bulk, in a black doctoral robe stepping up into the pulpit, he appeared mountainous. He could thunder; he could tell stories that made you laugh till you wept, and then he could make you weep for empathy. His sermons were compositional masterpieces and his oral delivery the envy of any preacher. He had something like a small degree of fame in Presbyterian circles. Some young men who lived with him told me that he loved to sit in the center of a room with a world-class stereo, with his eyes closed, and listen to a Beethoven symphony at full blast. This is fitting. To listen to a Thielemann sermon was a bit like sitting directly a few feet away from an orchestra performing a Beethoven symphony—it might plaster your hair straight back. To say the effect was powerful is laughable understatement. It was more like being strapped to the exterior of a supersonic jet plane in flight.

With Bruce, I left behind the pale, Anglo, ink and watercolor Jesus of the Sunday school literature in exchange for "Christ the tiger." This was actually one of his sermon titles and the sermon was as thrilling as the title suggests. Jesus was a man, probably looking like a current day Palestinian, speaking Aramaic and *not* Elizabethan English, who challenged the Pharisees and Sadducees and whipped the money changers out of the temple. He was no pansy, but a god/man who knew his own mind. He told the rich young ruler to leave behind his wealth and follow. I saw the squirming in the pews as Bruce delivered Christ's teachings on riches on occasion. American Christianity loves to ignore Christ's teachings on Mammon and the dangers of wealth. What does that say about us? Yet, this tiger, Christ the Tiger, also held off a mob about to stone a woman and forgave her. He forgave the weeping woman who washed his feet and in turn rudely pointed out to the Pharisee host that she had been a better host than he. Jesus was rather a bull in the china shop of first century Palestine. But in his outstanding strength, his greatest strength was his ability to love the unlovable. My understanding grew with Bruce's illumination.

While he was at Glendale Presbyterian, he engaged in two campaigns, one of which was a resounding victory and the second which he resolved at last by a strategic retreat. The first campaign began on February 9, 1971. The San Fernando-Sylmar earthquake did tremendous damage across the Southland, as Angelenos refer to the general Los Angeles area. Specifically to my story, it shook the cathedral-castle of brick that was the Glendale Presbyterian Church and did everything but knock it down into rubble. It still stood, teetering, but the authorities condemned the building without hesitation. It was unsafe to enter. Bruce rose to the occasion like the commanding general he was and rallied the congregation emotionally and financially. We were compelled for almost two years to worship in the fellowship hall and gym, but Bruce made even this somehow majestic. One of his many fundraising strategies was to enlist the church's top-rate choir to put on a Christmas festival of feasting and traditional music called "The Hanging of the Greens." Bruce sat in the middle, dressed in Renaissance costume, looming like Henry VIII over the festivities. What had been a gym took on the mystique of a grand Renaissance hall thereafter in whatever events were held in it. The money and enthusiasm flowed. In short order, the new church rose and stands there today.

Bruce's second battle I see clearer in hindsight now, though I only had hints from overhearing my parents discuss it at the time. A few years before Bruce arrived, Barry Goldwater set the Republican Party on a direction that is still prevalent today. I don't wish to discuss all of that here, but the merging of conservative politics and Evangelical Christianity in the minds of many was well underway by the time Bruce came to lead Glendale Presbyterian in 1968. Though many Presbyterians are mainstream, there had always been a strong Evangelical element at Glendale, probably as a result of it being in the middle of a conservative, white community. Bruce was a product of a seminary in his native Pennsylvania affiliated with the United Presbyterian branch. That branch and that seminary reflected a more moderate understanding of Christian faith that owed little to tent meetings and Baptist theology, as did the Evangelical tradition. So the battle lines were invisibly drawn the day Bruce walked in the front door. As I said, Bruce had little patience for nonsense and the idea that Christianity might be the same thing as conservatism would necessarily have set him instantly into battle mode. Other witnesses to the tensions through the end of Bruce's tenure have cited his tactlessness in staff relations and his spending priorities as reasons for his eventual leaving. And doubtless, that is true as far as it goes. But I clearly remember sermons Bruce gave that went against the Evangelical understanding and watching people I knew to be conservatives stiffen in their pews. Bruce loved firing a volley into opposing ranks. I suspect it thrilled him. And he did not suffer fools gladly. The battle was joined.

The second thing that Bruce did for me, after teaching me about Christ the Tiger, was teach me freedom from a prescribed left or right view of the world. For Bruce's Christianity was not liberal, though he was accused of that by people on the far right, who saw anyone left of them as radical, socialist communists. Bruce had no patience either for those liberal theologians and theologies that dismissed the supernatural events in the Bible in an ill-advised attempt to make nice with materialist philosophy, and all theologies that scorned the possibility of the miraculous. Bruce liked to thunder from the pulpit that Jesus Christ was risen from the dead, and no mistake; there was nothing "merely metaphorical" about it—it was primary fact. Christ the Tiger had roared and leaped from the grave. There was quite a bit of the firm assertion of Karl Barth in him, though while I am certain he read Barth, I doubt that he was a Barthian. Bruce may have dipped liberally from the writings of great thinkers, but he was his own man, or rather he was Christ's man and no more. Bruce advocated no apologetic, cringing Christianity, tolerant to the point of dismissing itself in favor of all other religions. The Resurrection of Christ was and is the central fact of history and Bruce announced it boldly from the pulpit.

But his theology was not conservative either. He was no fundamentalist nor Evangelical (though sadly those two words have come in time to mean the same thing in many people's minds—a fact that overlooks how many Evangelicals are *not* conservative), and had little patience for the Baptist sort of theology which has since pervaded some Evangelical thought. He was no inerrantist on scripture. He had respect for the historical-critical method on biblical studies. Plus, Bruce was extremely well read.

My father started attending church for the first time in my life because with Bruce, Christianity was real for him for the first time. And both my father and I were drawn to this Christianity that had respect for the mind, and for science, and what it had discovered, and did not hide in a paranoid hole from the realities of the world that might conflict with an inflexible, traditional reading of scripture. From Bruce I learned that one could believe in Christ, honor truth, and think with all the powers of one's mind without fear of being a heretic. One could move past the pale, smiling, Anglo, ink and watercolor Jesus and ride on the back of Christ the Tiger. Bruce especially was no respecter of what we now call the "prosperity gospel" and offended the conservatives in the congregation by suggesting that Christ meant what he said about rich men having difficulty getting into Heaven. He preached boldly that we are in fact our brother's keeper, and that no reciting variations on the phrase "personal responsibility" lets us off the hook as followers of Christ when it comes to serving the poor. These were Bruce's "heresies" and they have been mine ever since. Indeed, if you were to accuse me of having "Thielemannic theology," I would plead guilty. He made me a "mere" Christian, neither liberal nor conservative. He gave me reasons to find my faith in a place different than the regimented lockstep of Mr. M and Paul Harvey. Had he not done so, I probably would not have stayed with the pale, ink and watercolor Sunday school Jesus past my teen years. But of course, in doing so, Bruce made me a "heretic."

Increasingly "heresy" was in part being defined by many in that church at that time as not being Republican, not supporting candidates like Richard Nixon, which came to the same thing as not being Evangelical. Christianity and conservative were more and more being merged in the public perception. My own parents were Democrats in a vastly Republican town, and with other more intellectual families, such as the Polhemuses, we were the support and friends of Bruce at Glendale Presbyterian as his war with the Evangelical Right heated up over time. I was in high school by the time Bruce's war came to a head. I will save that for the next chapter. But not only did Bruce give me the freedom to be a thinking Christian, neither left nor right—he gave me Jack.

I can safely say that to this day, Bruce Thielemann was and is my spiritual father. And he introduced me to my other spiritual father, C.S. "Jack" Lewis. The formal introduction to Lewis came later. Here in junior high, Bruce's mention of the *Chronicles of Narnia* caused my parents to buy them for me. One school day I had the great, good fortune to wake up and find I had a severe flu. I was confined to bed with only the *Chronicles of Narnia* at hand. Oh, happy fate! My poor, wracked body languished for a week. That was fine—I wasn't using it at the moment. My mind was off to Narnia. I consumed two books per day for two and a half days and when I'd finished *The Last Battle*, I was bitterly disappointed that the series had ended. A generation later, kids reading Harry Potter had somewhat the same experience. And I since that time, I have had the experience again reading Tolkien. But that first trip to Narnia blew my mind, blew my heart, and soaked me in joy and longing like I've rarely known.

Six: High School and Farewell to California

No man thinks there is much ado about nothing when the ado is about himself

—*The Bertrams*, Anthony Trollope

I realize in looking back over what I've written, that I've neglected perhaps the primary point that all this might have to you, the reader. The age that started in politics with Goldwater slowly infected American thought with what I wish to call the Binary Imperative. In politics, increasingly one was either a liberal or a conservative. You had to buy *all* the narrative. The gap grew wider and angrier after the Carter and Reagan administrations to the point that news sources here in 2016 report that moderates have almost ceased to exist. Sadly, because of the merging of much (not all) of Evangelical Christianity and conservatism starting back in my youth, the same Binary Imperative certainly infected American Christianity as well. Bruce would have thought, and I still do think, that all of this is bewilderingly obtuse. I don't like to buy package deals for television, real estate or travel. Let me choose the details. Most Americans don't like package deals. Yet, we will embrace one political stance and then, though we haven't really thought about them, we absorb the rest of the political or philosophical stances that are popularly sold with them in one package deal. Thus someone who initially votes Republican because he or she in deeply examined conscience believes that abortion is murder, comes to reject climate science without so much as bothering to read the actual reports, because "their side" rejects it and Fox TV tells them so. It has often been remarked how conservatism today, unlike the Buckley era conservatism, has not so much embraced ignorance as "anti-knowledge." The feeling among American conservatives that the world has changed so fast that they must deny obvious truths before them that seem to threaten their traditional beliefs, sadly is going a long way to de-evangelize America. Anything outside their narrative is assumed to be a threat and a lie, so they bury their heads in the conservative narrative and tell the rest of us we're going to hell if we don't join them. This sort of thing drives away millennials in droves. If conservatives had sat down and said to themselves, "What can we do to cause America to reject Christ?" they couldn't have done a better job. Some of my conservative friends are bewildered that their arguments against abortion and homosexuality find so little hearing among millennials. But what they don't understand is that in the eyes of millennials, when conservatives rant against government helping the poor, they have surrendered the moral high ground that would have given them any hope of making a moral case. And when conservatives turn a blind eye to the reality of climate science, in the eyes of millennials they have surrendered any possibility of claiming to have any respect for the truth. Thus, conservative beliefs, based mainly in economics, have poisoned any witness conservative Christians have for Christ in the eyes of much of the coming generation.

Of course, there are liberals who do just as much damage. When one Episcopalian bishop, whom I shall not name, announces that Christianity is just one of many world religions, no more valuable than the rest, and that the miraculous events in Christianity are just metaphors, he does just as much to drive away believers and de-evangelize America. Why we feel that we must embrace the Liberal Binary Imperative or the Conservative Binary Imperative is beyond me. Perhaps it's a side effect to the strategic side of politics, that seeks to bind together coalitions with differing views in order to dominate the vote. But it is an abdication of moral thinking on the part of the individual. Like Bruce, I find each issue deserves its own close examination, and like Bruce, I find myself with little company in the vast no man's land between two warring camps of True Believers, left and right, who have bought package deals.

But the more I think of it, the more I think there is to it. As I taught my college students, we all start from assumptions. Author Stephen Prothero (no relation to me that I know of) writes in his book *Why Liberals Win the Culture Wars (Even When they Lose Elections)*, that conservatism is ultimately about trying to save already lost causes, that conservatives start to fight their battles when the outcome has already been determined. So they are forever in their narrative fighting a rearguard action for lost causes. This only causes more isolation and unwillingness to consider facts that may run contrary to the narrative. If you don't agree with the narrative, as happened with climate science, you are dismissed as liberals and liars.

Bruce faced the first small waves of this coming tsunami in his battle at Glendale Presbyterian. In high school I got to know him better and to speak privately to him on several occasions. I became one of several young people he took an interest in. He lived in a house with several young men as roommates, many of whom subsequently became ministers like him. And I grew in many new directions in that church. I entered Glendale High School in the fall of 1971. There, a friend of mine had dragged me into rock n' roll and I learned bass guitar. I played several times for the church, a service that gave me much sense of direction and fulfillment. To a large degree I was unaware at the time of the increasing tensions Bruce had to deal with, though I had hints from overhearing my parents discuss the issues. So I was astonished when he announced his resignation. Around me I heard some people rejoicing that the "leftist" preacher was leaving. Others, like me ,were dismayed and sorry. My parting gift to him was an oil painting I had made exactly like the one described in the opening scene of *The Voyage of the Dawn Treader* of the *Chronicles of Narnia*. He was very pleased with it and it hung in his office in later years. But all this happened near the end of my high school days. Bruce was there to provide the spiritual open door for me till I graduated, leaving a few months later to take a position in his home state of Pennsylvania.

High school itself for me was an improvement on junior high. I was still unathletic and awkward, but as each year went by I found good friends. There was always Gregg, and now another friend, Jim Thorburn, who was keyboard player in the band that competed against mine. Thorburn and I would record things on his reel to reel tape recorder, hanging microphones from ceiling lamps and using other jury-rigged techniques that we referred to as "mickey mouse" techniques to make up for our lack of proper equipment. He drove an MG sports car and riding in it was a blast. However, he spent about 50% of his time with the car with the hood open trying to get it to run. Thorburn's endless repair jobs on used sports cars became somewhat his trademark. I once told him that if I walked into his house and didn't see a sports car in pieces in the garage, I would think he was an impostor. He later became a professional musician, and later an attorney in Colorado. He still has a car in pieces in his garage in Colorado; I've seen it—all is well.

My friend Richard Stillwell, whom I met at church, was an aspiring Jimmy Page (guitarist of Led Zeppelin for those who didn't know) , and as I already mentioned, he talked me into learning bass, mainly for his own reasons. I played in his band for something like two years. Whatever motives Richard had for recruiting me, it opened up a fresh new world to me and gave me a way to know other people and break out of my shyness. For me bass, and later guitar, were a road out of introversion.

Here too, I had some great teachers: Al Koerner taught me history and government and I've never forgotten the assertion he made with a sigh, that if you gave the average American his job, house, and beer, he'd go along with anything you wanted to propose. My greatest teacher was Julie Davies, later a successful professor at Fullerton College. She gave me a grounding in literature that moved away from a static understanding to a dynamic one in which we could see what literature had to do with life. She was as significant a teacher to me in literature and writing as Saul Cohen had been in art.

My senior year, as often happens, (as a veteran high school teacher I've observed this every year for years in my own students) was a revolution from my other two. I was in a band, so people knew me and talked to me and didn't care if I wasn't in a sport. My dating life was almost non-existent, but a pretty girl consented to go to prom with me. I had my useless crushes on girls, but they passed. I was on the yearbook staff and worked as a photographer and writer, a thoroughly enjoyable experience. And this year of 1974 was the year that streaking became the latest fad. Most of the streakers caught on campus (they invariably seemed to get caught) were in student government, an interesting concept the longer I think about it.

My painting gave way to more writing and it was years till my art resurfaced. I graduated in June of 1974, and my graduation was streaked, which seemed wholly fitting to me. I felt out of place in Glendale. I had road fever and the desire to go to college all at the same time. Gregg too graduated and went to Caltech, where his brilliance could be really challenged. My band with Richard broke up. Bruce went back to Pennsylvania. After a year of drifting through community college, I made the decision to go to school in the mountains of Arizona, at Northern Arizona University, right smack dab in the middle of the magical country I had traveled to as a boy. My grandparents had left me and my brothers enough money for a full ride through college. The quasi-Narnian magic of the Four Corners Country drew me, as well as the growing realization that my dear, sweet, overprotective mother, would never let me grow up if I didn't put some distance between her and me. I left Glendale in the summer of 1975 and never returned except as a visitor to the town where I was born.

I could not overstate the joyful revolution that living in the high forests and studying literature was to me. I could write a separate book on how I exploded in growth at Northern Arizona, and how Flagstaff became for me, as much a hometown as Glendale. I now tell people I was born in Glendale but I grew up in Flagstaff. I remember feeling psychologically like a pre-teen because of my mother's insistence that my brothers and I did not exhibit adolescent behavior. When I reached Flagstaff, I released like a spring set free. At first, I tried to get involved with a church youth group, but after a few weeks I let this pass and ceased to attend any sort of church-related activity. Somewhere in that first semester of freedom I came upon my "blank slate" experience. And I'm now convinced that the fact that the programs I tried to access were all Evangelical acted as a turn-off to me. Bruce had taught me the freedom of the mind from the puritanical approach of conservative Evangelicalism and I didn't like the taste of it anymore.

All this is not unusual. Often young people raised in faith come to question it as they reach college age. They have to make the world their own, and not just a clone of their parents'. That was true for me. And if nothing else, at that time of life one is free to explore forbidden territory, and that pull affected me as well. But I wasn't one to just toss the pharisaical restrictions of youth and go joyfully plunging into alcohol, sex and drugs, as is very common. For one thing I hadn't the puritanical Evangelical restrictions to rebel against—I had known Christ the Tiger. Secondly, all the meds I'd had to take for my ADD had given me a serious distrust of drugs, legal or otherwise. Marijuana seemed to mainly aggravate my hay fever and make me headachy and nauseous, so I didn't much enjoy it. Then-popular comedian Bill Cosby used to have a story in which in his college years he found himself drunk in a dirty bar bathroom, puking his guts out and asking himself, "This is fun?" I was aware of the story when the exact same thing happened to me and I asked the exact same question. The answer pretty much made the prospect of getting seriously drunk unappealing to me up till this day.

As for sex, my dating life improved and I had a few hot and quick romantic failures. But what I couldn't bring myself to do, which so many of the guys in my dorm did so freely (and loved to brag about), was to bed a girl for a night or three and then toss her off. Perhaps it was the vision of my parents' marriage or some sense of chivalry I held onto, but the idea of using a woman repelled me. I couldn't bring myself to do it.

Most importantly to this account, I walked away from my faith. But I didn't reject it outright. I approached the whole thing like a referee. I cleaned the slate and invited God to write on it. I would be open-minded and consider the evidence as it came forth. He took seven years to go about writing on my slate, but he did. More importantly during this time, I wrote all my doubts and thoughts in long letters to Bruce and he wrote long letters back. Each letter of his clarified my mind. Christ may have been the Tiger, but in those years he stalked me slowly and gently, waiting to pounce in love and not force. I did not see him crouched in the grass, but he was there.

I had a history of really good best friends over the years. Nigel, though our friendship resumed later in life, at this time was off into his own rebellion against his parents and his complete mastery of the electric guitar. I found him again later on down the line. Gregg was at Caltech and then off on various jobs, ending up in Seattle, where I still see him from time to time. But there in that first semester, I met a tall, blond, bearded dude with glasses, a fellow English major named Bob Frederick. Our history would fill its own book, but I will say that soon we were trekking all over the Holy Four Corners Country in his blue, 1973 Econoline van he'd named "Tarkus", after a character off an ELP album cover. And like me, Bob had been raised Christian and was now questioning his faith. We forged a bond of voluntary brotherhood that lasted until cancer took him in 2014. As I said, I could write volumes about Bob, but that's not the focus here. The principal thing he did for me then was that he was on the same spiritual walk, but he'd been out in the world a lot longer. So like a big brother, he guided me. And Bob was an Anglican, an Episcopalian. This was the first time I had been exposed to that balanced form of Christianity. In later years, this became very important.

Also in that second year I fell deeply and really in love with a girl that was extremely compatible to all things I valued. She was an artist, a lover of the outdoors, about my own temperament, and though I didn't see it at the time, her Catholic Christianity drew me. But the relationship broke up after a month and a half. Still, this girl had set an earthquake going in my heart. For a full decade afterwards, all the relationships I had or might have had were haunted by the knowledge that there were women out there completely compatible with me, and that the woman standing before me wasn't one of them. It wasn't till I met my wife that I discovered that compatibility again. This long delay came to test my faith in God's plan for me. It took a decade, though I was impatient. I have found that God may be forgiving, and providing, but he does not feel compelled by our impatience.

My great tragedy was that by the end of my second year, my best roommate, Larry Begay, my best friend, Bob, and my best girlfriend had all left me. By the end of spring semester 1977 I was as alone at NAU as the day I walked in. Bob was uncertain what to do with college—in hindsight he should have changed his major to vocal music—and Larry was no longer funded by the Navajo tribe. He went and got a construction job. And the girl that came the closest to my heart more than any before and on for another decade after, had returned to her high school boyfriend. I spent a year and a half more at Northern Arizona, but I never found friendship or love of that quality again for the whole time I was there. I was in the middle of a place as close to earthly paradise as I could get, but I was getting more lonely, restless and ready to ramble.

Seven: Rambling and Joy

Not until we are lost do we begin to understand ourselves.

—Henry David Thoreau

As much as I had loved Flagstaff and NAU, by the time graduation arrived in December of 1978, I was so jaded I just left and did not show up for the commencement ceremony the following June. Looking back on it now, I see it as one of several blind places I had in my infinite 23 year old wisdom. I still believed that the grass actually was greener over the next fence and the next fence and the next fence, *ad infinitum*. It was something I now call joylust. I was infinitely patient with people and irrationally impatient with everything else. I still am. It is one of my greatest faults. I really, honestly thought that if I played my cards right, I could line up all those experiences of joy that I found in backpacking, in nature, in travel, even in relationship with a woman I truly loved, and live a sort of permanent high till my dying day. And it was a Rocky Mountain high. I was in love with that country. If the reader is laughing at me here, it is just. I marvel even today that my commitment to denial was so powerful that it took decades to break free of it. As part and parcel of that denial, I could not believe my father's gentle admonition that if I wanted to live somewhere, I needed a job. I had graduated college and wanted to be a novelist. Menial jobs made me frustrated and impatient. I almost think now that I expected someone to hire me as a novelist and give me a generous paycheck on spec. Of course, the book trade does not operate like that and I well knew it. But in further hindsight I recognize now that I was always the artist, and that I just had no idea how to pursue or define it.

My answer to all this? Ramble down the road. I will not try here to construct the correct sequence of rambles, temporary jobs in environmental education (a job a friend got me and the only one I seemed to be able to stand), landings at my parents' house in San Clemente (for the simple reason that it was the one place I got free meals and a bed), followed by further rambles. I call this time my "Jackson Browne Phase." I was truly running on empty and running blind, running into the sun, and running behind. I was chasing joy or happiness or something I couldn't name down the highway. But anyone who has had this experience well knows that what you chase is like a mirage on a desert highway: it recedes and recedes before you on the horizon. Part of the reason I've always loved Jackson Browne's early music was because it was as if he were writing the sound track to my life in those years.

My most prolonged ramble was in the summer following graduation, the summer of 79. I sold my good 67 Mustang fastback (one of the principal acts I'd take back if I could now) for a crappy Datsun pickup with a camper-back, loaded my backpacking gear, non-perishable food and my guitar, and headed to the Rocky Mountains. I had a vague plan that when I stumbled on Rocky Mountain Paradise, I would just stay. But that was just the problem. Whatever I was chasing, it was always on the horizon. I found myself hungry to keep moving and unable to stay and enjoy any place or anything. My little truck was the ideal backpacking base. I had imagined that given my fascination with the early days of the Rocky Mountains, the fur trade and the Indians, that I would love solo backpacking and was a loner just waiting to be set free. Wrong! I became people-starved quite rapidly. I backpacked almost nowhere. I discovered painfully that I was no loner. One event I still look back on and wonder at my own foolishness, was when I met a gorgeous waitress in Jackson Hole who hinted that maybe I could stay around a few days. This was after I'd written her a love note on a napkin and she'd caught me before I went out the door. Idiot that I was, I told her no and rambled on. It's a girl, my lord in a flatbed Ford and I missed it! So much for finding paradise and staying. If a pretty girl in Jackson Hole wasn't paradise enough, I didn't really know what was. But I was grasping desperately for that thing, whatever it was, that always receded on the horizon. I ended up taking in 12,600 miles of the US and Canada before I was done. And almost every mile of it was desperately lonely. My dream ramble turned into a bitter lesson about myself.

At some point I found myself in Detroit with my best friend Bob again and we spent a week together traveling around Michigan. By this point I had come up with a plan. I was going to settle in Santa Fe. I talked Bob into meeting me there. He committed to following me within a month. Then I left him and went to see Bruce Thielemann in western Pennsylvania, where he was chaplain at Grove City College. He was actually rather severe with me and in so many words told me I was a fool in my pointless rambling. Bruce was always small on tact and big on truth. He was entirely correct, of course. I rambled on, more confused than ever but committed to my Santa Fe plan.

I arrived in Santa Fe, but my resolve foundered on the same impatience I had with menial jobs. Within a month, I moved on to Flagstaff and met Bob there instead. I worked delivering pizza. I made a halfhearted attempt at getting an English teaching credential in Arizona and started a short-lived rock band named Sweet Medicine. Both failed within two months. By Christmas, I did something I regret to this day—I left Bob by himself in Flagstaff and went back to California to work in environmental education again, a job I could tolerate. And leaving Bob I still look back on as a betrayal, though he never faulted me for it. He forgave quickly and thoroughly.

Here is where I want to reach back to the issue of joy. So far in this narrative there has been more than one axis: the first is my life and the second is the issue of faith. Here we have a third and equally important axis: joy and joylust. I say that because though truth is vital, and my life might mildly amuse the reader, if you keep reading I believe the main reason is that you've experienced this wild, powerful thing C.S. Lewis and I have called joy.

Lewis admitted that "I sometimes wonder if all pleasures are not substitutes for Joy." (*Surprised* 170) The longer I live the more I believe Lewis was correct on this point. I once wrote a character in a novel named Eddie. Eddie was a totally physical and athletic person, a football star, a Marine, a womanizer, and later in life, a wife abuser. And yet Eddie wanted that something that everyone feels is lacking. For someone like me or Lewis, this random and powerful euphoria comes to us in the beauty of art and nature. But I believe Lewis' suspicions are right, that all of us, whether by the thrill of gridiron collisions, the thrill of excessive speed, or for that matter any sort of adrenaline-pumping physical thrill, are substitutes for Joy. This becomes more universal and profound when I think that all those who, knowing the dangers, get into powerful drugs, doing it on the off chance of finding a substitute for Joy that performs on command.

One friend I know writes Christian apologetics that appeal to reason. But I believe a large part of the reason Lewis has a wide following when most Christian apologetic writers don't, is that he moves beyond reason to address this hunger in each person's soul. Thoreau wrote that "most men lead lives of quiet desperation . . . . " If Lewis and I are right, though there may be war, tragedy, and starvation, for most people trying to bring back that euphoric moment of meaningfulness is the supreme effort. We often stick it on something we think we want, feeling that we will have it when we get what we want. I did this with relationships, thinking that when I had a girlfriend, then I'd be happy much the same way I thought what I wanted was just up the road a few miles. This accounts for many of the failures in my early romances; the reality didn't live up to the crazy, desperate hope. Much of our consumerism and our other addictions, like gambling, or obsessing over a hobby, are at bottom, this search for a way to reproduce that crazy, addicting experience of Joy.

Lewis himself eventually came to conclude that it was just a signpost, a hint of Heaven meant to draw us that direction. For a long time, though I found myself in agreement with Lewis elsewhere, I found this dismissal to be somehow inadequate.

But I think any recovered alcoholic, or drug user, or gambler, or for that matter, anyone who has fought the demons of addiction, they know that turning and walking away, every day of the rest of your life is the only road to sanity. Lewis wasn't so wrong. One has to turn away from the draw of addiction to the rest of one's life. And this hint of Heaven, Joy, is so powerful, can itself trigger other addiction. It's a sobering thought. And it's pivotal. For what we conclude about how to deal with this powerful, drawing urge makes a lot of difference whether we're going to be a satisfied or dissatisfied Christian, a perennially disappointed lover, an addicted gambler, or a drug casualty.

Eight: Jack Lewis Surprises Me

> What distressed me most—more even than my own folly—was the perplexing question, How can beauty and ugliness dwell so near?
>
> —*Phantastes*, George MacDonald

So I was back in California, more confused than ever. Everything I had placed in the vacuum my Christianity had left behind had evaporated and proved itself a mirage. Looking back on it now, I would with the benefit of hindsight, have realized, that 1) I was some sort of artist and needed to find a way to live that, and 2) being an artist meant doing something else likely menial for money to survive on at least in the early and middle stages if one were lucky. But I did not know nor want to believe such things. I got into a messy and short-lived romance that ended my career in environmental education. That door closed, but I had discovered that I could bear jobs that involved teaching. With my background in environmental education, I took some teacher aide jobs in my parents' town. Somehow teaching did not engage my frustration and sense of futility as had any other job. I should have taken this as a clue to my true calling, but I was still in the fog of denial and in no hurry to emerge.

There I was, sitting in a bedroom in my parents' house, with little money, an English degree, and no direction. I was 24 years old going on 25 and all that I had dreamed of since college had been hastily abandoned in my impatience, or had self-destructed, like my music career. I had finished a novel of mixed quality and even I knew it wasn't all that good. It was titled, *The Sun is But a*

Morning Star, a title I took from the final line of Thoreau's *Walden*. Looking back, it seems comically presumptuous for a 24 year old, confused young man to pontificate about the meaning of life in a novel. That nobody took me or my novel seriously in retrospect is hardly surprising. This is the point where the Tiger leaped from the brush and grabbed me by the heart and the mind. It came about when I stumbled "accidentally" on a C.S. Lewis book my mom had lying around. It was a book they'd bought years before to give to Donald, on Bruce's suggestion when Don was struggling with faith in his high school years. Since then it had collected dust. I read it, and if someone had hit me on the side of the head with a baseball bat, the shock would have been less. It was *Surprised by Joy*.

The Tiger had not been idle over the years. Before I left NAU, I felt the explanation of human behavior in terms of the fall of humanity in sin fit the facts better than any sort of psychological theory. Psychology does a contorted dance around the question of good and evil, which it knows it cannot define. But to believe that all evil can be explained away with psychological explanations is a fools' game and I'd come to realize it. Psychology was fine so long as it stayed in its narrow confines of explaining large swaths of known human behavior. When it tried to be as large as philosophy or theology, it became laughable.

I also came to feel that Jesus of Nazareth really was more than a country preacher, misconstrued by his followers and executed by the Roman government. I wasn't sure where that was going, but the minimalist explanation didn't fly. Thus the Tiger had made two critical moves to place himself in position to pounce.

And to pounce on me, he sent C.S. "Jack" Lewis. Lewis I had met vaguely in his *Chronicles of Narnia*—and looking back on it now, there wasn't much difference between Christ the Tiger and Christ the Lion. But *Surprised by Joy* was Jack's spiritual autobiography, his Augustinian confession. What struck me with such force is that though Lewis was raised in Belfast and suffered through English boarding schools, and never set foot in America, much less the Southwest and the Rocky Mountains, he had been struck with joy in the precise manner that I had. He too mounted a fruitless chase and was a victim of joylust. He was the literary artist and in his early days, visual artist too, the non-athletic boy shunned by his schoolmates for his inability to play games well. Though it seemed impossible, in spite of all the differences of circumstance, time, and nation, Jack had grown up just like me. The only significant difference I could discern was that he had lost his mother early and unlike me had resorted to a virulent pessimism and atheism. I had just found my freedom and resorted to an open-minded agnosticism. But piece by piece, Jack worked his way back to faith. I was willing to do so too, but all my intellectual problems stood in the way. And this is what Jack Lewis did for me and for many others too. With clarity and simplicity, Lewis honestly and openly confronted all the intellectual objections to faith, all the road-blocks, and plowed right through them.

By the end of the book, the road back to faith was clear of obstructions. I know the Evangelical reader would want me to say I knelt down and prayed. Well, I prayed, even if I didn't do it the prescribed way. I was probably sitting in a chair with the book half-open in my hands. Heck, Lewis prayed his surrender prayer in the sidecar of a motorcycle. I didn't need the emotional Evangelical kneel. The important thing was that I admitted Christ was God and knew I had to live accordingly.

Some Evangelical readers will be tempted to put the book down at this point. After all, I've been "saved," end of story. No, no, no. As I said before, our being saved, our being changed (as Lewis pointed out) into the sort of person Christ meant us to be when we were created, that takes a long, long time. Conversion is a process, not a moment. This was only the start. I have yet to see the finish.

Now the reader may question my math, because earlier I said that the Tiger had taken seven years to get me back, and this is 1980 and I've only been out of the sheepfold for five. True enough. My heart was home and my intellect was satisfied for the time being. But joylust is something like an addiction. Maybe it is in fact an addiction. I was still struggling in the Tiger's maw.

Meanwhile, over the next three years I bought and read everything Lewis wrote, except perhaps for some of the critical studies over books I hadn't read. And he never disappointed. He was balanced like Bruce, neither liberal nor conservative, though many try to claim him for one side or another by cherry-picking him. In fact, I became something of a Lewis scholar. By 1985, I had discovered and joined the Southern California C.S. Lewis Society, which proved to be an open door to many worlds.

I suppose it could be said that Jack and I thought so much alike that it was natural for me to see life in his terms without much discomfort. And if you find Lewis' world-view repugnant, you can toss this book in the return pile now. But be sure you do that for what Lewis is and not what someone told you he is. Let me make six points as to why I was so influenced by Lewis so readily.

1. Lewis neither right nor left

It is pretty universally known that C.S. Lewis in creating Puddleglum, the marshwiggle in *The Chronicles of Narnia*, was modeling the pessimistic-optimist character of the creature on the personality of his gardener, Fred Paxford. As much as this is true, in a far subtler sense, Lewis was creating, perhaps unconsciously, with Puddleglum, an image of himself. It's like we're all human, but Jack Lewis is a marshwiggle. And that marshwiggle thinking, so very marshwiggelian in it's consistency and character, is startling and arresting to those of us who aren't marshwiggles.

In *The Silver Chair*, Puddleglum starts off as being merely the pessimist. If Lewis had kept the characterization of Puddleglum along these lines, Puddleglum would have been merely an interesting but marginal character. But Puddleglum grows in the course of the story, and becomes a projection of Lewis' own personality, or perhaps more accurately, Lewis' thinking.

Puddleglum's acts in the prince's quarters are both surprising and brimming with courage and integrity. He insists on freeing the prince from the silver chair when the sign is given, even if following the sign means certain death. But his magnum opus is Puddleglum's magnificent analysis of the witch's argument after he has just stomped out her magical fire. What's unique about this analysis is that it starts with what sound like concessions. Puddleglum allows for the witch's version of reality. He's all about anticipating counter-argument. But then he turns that reality on its head by arguing that the imaginary world is better than the "real" one and worth fighting and dying for. This piece of what seems like pretzel logic the witch cannot answer and she resorts to combat instead.

All these actions of Puddleglum are far above and beyond mere pessimism. They take us by surprise. They are contrary to our expectations. And they reflect the way that Lewis defeats his critics' expectations repeatedly.

As one example of this, Lewis' approach to literary criticism was simultaneously reactionary and revolutionary. In the face of the school of F.R. Leavis and I.A. Richards, Lewis not only attacked Modernist approaches to literature, he undercut their ground so that they simply were irrelevant.

In the field of theology, despite his orthodox stance, Lewis can be maddeningly hard to pin down. Evangelicals are likely to criticize Lewis for not holding that the Bible is without error. Yet he reveres the Bible as scripture. He straddles the inerrancy debate. In *Reflections on the Psalms* he writes:

> His [Christ's] teaching therefore cannot be grasped by the intellect alone, cannot be "got up" as if it were a "subject". If we try to do that with it, we shall find Him the most elusive of teachers. He hardly ever gave a straight answer to a straight question. He will not be, in the way we want, "pinned down". The attempt is (again, I mean no irreverence) like trying to bottle a sunbeam.[1]

And as Lewis speaks of Christ's propensity to not be "pinned down," so Lewis the marshwiggle won't be pinned down either. This is the surprising marshwiggelian perspective emerging here. We want Lewis to be an inerrantist, or a Catholic, or an American Evangelical, or at least *something* with a firm position. We want him to try to bottle the sunbeam *somewhere* for Heaven's sake! He refuses to do it. He zigs when we look for him to zag.

1. Lewis, *Reflection on the Psalms*, 112-3.

One fares no better if one tries to pin Lewis down in terms of contemporary politics. In one essay in *God In the Dock* Lewis can bemoan becoming "willing slaves of the welfare state," a snarky title to warm the heart of any modern conservative or libertarian. Then he blows it all away in the next essay about how "We Have no Right to Happiness" that shoots down the underpinnings of libertarian thought. He places in his autobiography George MacDonald's assertion that the doorway to Hell is covered by the words "I am my own." Those words are perhaps the very heart of the libertarian concept and Lewis associates them with damnation. He applauds the concept of membership and disparages the concept of the collective, and yet in a personal letter concedes that the National Health Service is ultimately a good thing. For anybody uncertain of what that means, Lewis is mildly lauding a single-payer-system of socialized medicine, something which is an anathema to current day conservatives. With Tolkien, he deplores the mechanized future—I am certain he would have viewed the advent of the internet with horror—and embraces an almost Luddite agenda that would make any extremist eco-saboteur happy. Lewis calls himself conservative on more than one occasion, but when he is called on to describe the Christian state in *Mere Christianity*, it sounds at one time socially conservative and socialist.

> If there were such a [Christian] society in existence and you or I visited it, I think we should have come away with a curious impression. We should feel that its economic life was very socialistic and, in that sense, "advanced," but that it family life and its code of manners were rather old-fashioned—perhaps even ceremonious and aristocratic.[2]

On the next page of the same text, rather than embracing the sanctity of personal property, he tells us that if our giving does not make us uncomfortable, we're not giving enough. That means that in Lewis' view, it's not enough to look at the poor and recite the mantra of "personal responsibility." That is irrelevant; if our charities aren't making an uncomfortable dent in our precious

2. Lewis, *Mere Christianity*, 66.

prosperity, they are not enough. Lewis, in marshwiggelian ways, is not a liberal nor a conservative—rather someone who looks at all things honestly and objectively and often in surprising ways. I found this to be supremely liberating.

2. Honesty

Part of the reason Lewis engaged me so quickly was because he had nothing to sell. I don't know why in America we seem to feel the need to couch evangelization in the same language that we use to sell used cars. Much of this is tone as much as anything else. But like many Americans, when someone comes at me hard, determined to win me over, I assume they are a liar and want my money at any cost. I'll grant you that, given America's tent-evangelism heritage, many people are drawn in by the hard-sell approach to spreading the Gospel. Our megachurches are proof of that; our various corrupt and wealthy TV evangelists across the years are proof that if we are smart, we are wary. But most people aren't as smart as they could be and so wolves take in the sheep over TV programs or in megachurches, pushing the prosperity gospel and raking in the money. It is a sad legacy of American culture. We seem almost determined to be lied to. And yet the very same people will disbelieve climate change because they can be convinced that every climate scientist is liberal and therefore automatically a liar.

Lewis, perhaps in part because he was English, exuded none of this approach. If the evidence went against his position, he looked at it fairly and with due consideration. Never was I made to feel that I was being railroaded, in all the years I've read Lewis. One of my favorite quotes of his that exhibits this quality succinctly is: "I didn't go to religion to make me happy. I always knew a bottle of Port would do that. If you want a religion to make you feel really comfortable, I certainly don't recommend Christianity." (*God in the Dock* 48) In reading Lewis, I was reading an objective and detailed look at the old faith. Nothing short of this would have brought me back.

3. Clarity and humility

It is not because he is a skilled apologist that Lewis grabbed my attention. Lewis grabbed my attention because of his clarity, born principally from his skill at creating lucid metaphors, and his insistence on writing in plain English. Reading Lewis for many is like waking from sleep or clearing up a patch of mental fog—he was that for me. And he's so clear because Lewis understands that logic alone is not enough. We don't go to Lewis for logic—we go for clarity. We go for clarifying metaphors.

And the clarity, I later recognized as a writing teacher, is also created by Lewis' writing in either simple sentences, or complex sentences with not too many long clauses. His vocabulary is not ornate, not full of Greek or Latin-origin words that we have to go look up. And this goes back to how Lewis sees himself. The man was bloody brilliant, with two first degrees from Oxford and yet he was thoroughly convinced that Christ died for all men and that he was not to take on a sense of superiority or talk down to people. Instead he speaks honestly and simply, with no political agenda and no energy to convert nor conquer the reader. Part of the success of the Narnia stories is that this same humility extended to children. Another favorite quote of mine from an essay on how to write to children recounts how Lewis once said too loudly in a hotel dining room that he hated prunes:

> "So do I," came an unexpected six-year-old voice from another table.
>
> Sympathy was instantaneous. Neither of us thought it funny. We both knew that prunes are far too nasty to be funny. That is the proper meeting between man and child as independent personalities.[3]

It was also the proper meeting between person and person, but most importantly, writer and reader. I learned to trust him after a while. I have never found cause to regret that trust.

3. Lewis, *On Stories*, 42.

4. Lewis recognized the role of culture

As I mentioned before, I had long had a fascination with not only the Rockies and the opening of the far west, but with the Native American people who lived in those lands before the juggernaut of American settlement robbed them. While in college, I was allowed to design my own minor and so took *every* American history class, especially those having to do with the westward expansion and Native American history, and also every single anthropology class on Native American culture they offered. I only regret now that I didn't try to take Navajo language while I was there. And I came to have a large respect for the way that anthropology approaches culture. I also became aware of the vast disaster that missionization of the Native American people was in this country. White American missionaries came in with the understanding that they had the Bible and that their understanding of Christianity transcended all other cultures. Their culture was correct and all others weren't. Indeed, they probably didn't think of themselves as having a culture. They had the Gospel, their black clothes and puritan ways, and those were the ways of God. Or so they thought. And what they accomplished was to aid the destruction of those Native peoples and try to turn them into second-class citizens with the American version of Victorian values imposed on them. The racism, insensitivity, and complicity with the conquering armed forces of these missionaries were invisible to themselves, and it's a wonder that there are any Native American Christians at all in this country.

My knowledge of this was one of the barriers that impeded my return to Christianity. What was wonderfully liberating for me was Lewis' description of the natural law in *The Abolition of Man*. Lewis painted a view of the moral universe in which there was massive cultural variation, but within that there are universal moralities called the "natural law" by the Middle Ages. Then, instead of arguing from a position of cultural superiority of Western Culture, Lewis filled the book with examples of the synchronicity of natural law from times and cultures around the world.

In another place he addresses what happened in America during the westward expansion, as well as in the British Empire in the past, in the simple, succinct words: "Gun and Gospel have been horribly combined in the past." Anyone who tries to gloss over the American conquest of its native peoples will find no support in Lewis.

In yet another place he explained his concept of "chronological snobbery," a concept he got from Owen Barfield, as the idea that one's own time has all correct ideas and that the past is ignorant in all things automatically. Lewis held that each time and place had its characteristic insights and characteristic blindne sses and illusions. He wrote:

> In the first place [Barfield] made short work of what I have called my "chronological snobbery," the uncritical acceptance of the intellectual climate common to our own age and the assumption that whatever has gone out of date is on that account discredited. You must find why it went out of date. Was it ever refuted (and if so by whom, where, and how conclusively) or did it merely die away as fashions do? If the latter, this tells us nothing about its truth or falsehood. From seeing this, one passes to the realization that our own age is also "a period," and certainly has, like all periods, its own characteristic illusions. They are likeliest to lurk in those widespread assumptions which are so ingrained in the age that no one dares to attack or feels it necessary to defend them.[4]

It puzzles me today that even among the most intelligent of my Evangelical Lewis scholar friends, they hold a position that the current Evangelical consensus of the interpretation of the Bible is somehow transcendent above cultural bias, free from characteristic blindnesses and illusions of our own age. Lewis tells us that is not possible. We are no better nor worse than our ancestors. We have our cultural biases as surely as they did.

4. Lewis, *Suprised by Joy*, 207.

5. The expected use of our intelligence

I have been a high school teacher for thirty-two years now and a college instructor for twenty-six. So I find intelligence among people to be very unevenly distributed. Furthermore, I have come to believe in the theory of multiple intelligences, which would explain why the kid that struggles to write an essay is a genius on the football field. Still, as a teacher I have found that people are capable of thinking—if they do not succumb to laziness and really work at it. Sure, some people are going to run circles around others, but unless you are severely learning disabled, you can think clearly if you try. This is why I am puzzled that people buy pre-packaged philosophies like liberalism and conservatism, much less that they mistake one or the other for Christianity. This is clearly the influence of Bruce Thielemann on me and it was furthered by the influence of Jack Lewis. I too think like a marsh-wiggle. By that I mean every position is to be examined on its own merits, not shoved to one column or the other because Fox News or MSNBC like or dislike it. Most people don't seem to want to do this much mental work, which as a teacher does not surprise me. Pre-packaged is easier.

In *Mere Christianity* Lewis tells us that all our gifts are to be used, and that if we are Christian, Christ expects us to use all the intelligence we've got. For the Christian, intellectual laziness is as much a sin as any other type of laziness. This was a breath of fresh air to me. Here in America we have a long tradition of disparaging "smart people," "pointy heads," "poindexters," and "liberal intellectuals," and even fearing and distrusting people who think. This is a weakness in our national character and it does not serve us either individually nor collectively. As I've said, I have good friends in the world of Lewis scholarship who are Evangelical and deep thinkers. Sadly, they are the exception and not the rule in the conservative Evangelical world. This accounts for a lot of the push-back Bruce got at Glendale Presbyterian. Our American cultural value of distrusting intelligence is not a Christian value. It's the sin of sloth in fact. Lewis offered me a vision of Christianity free of that.

6. Imagination

As I said previously, I am a trained Romantics scholar. I was doubtlessly born a Romantic. I published a book, co-written with a friend, on Lewis' Romanticism and anyone who wants all the details and my theories can go there.[5] Here I'll just say that the Romantic in Lewis drew me. Not only was he a devotee of Joy like me, he loved nature, art, and beauty in the same way. I have known people who knew Lewis well, but I was seven when he died. Indeed, it was just a few days before I saw Oswald killed. But I think if Jack and I had met as adults, we would have found ourselves talking avidly very soon after meeting. I have encountered few other writers whose mind follows the same trails as my own so closely.

More importantly, perhaps Lewis' greatest intellectual achievement is that he found a balance between reason and romanticism. I won't get academic here, but my theory is that our Western Culture has swung on a pendulum between rationalist philosophies and movements, and romantic philosophies and movements. The 1780-1850 period in British literature was but one instance of this, not the only one. What Lewis does that no other writer I know has done, is he finds balance between these competing philosophies. In an essay he wrote "For me, reason is the natural organ of truth; but imagination is the organ of meaning. Imagination, producing new metaphors or revivifying old, is not the cause of truth, but its condition."[6] Put even more simply, reason, logic, and facts tell us what; imagination tells us why. Imagination answers the question of meaning. Reason and science answer the question of means. Neither are more nor less important than the other. But neither can we dispose of either. Thus, as George MacDonald had first engaged Lewis with his fantasy novel *Phantastes*, Lewis first engaged me with the *Chronicles of Narnia*. I got the meaning first and the means second, when I read Lewis' non-fiction. Because perhaps of my parents and the way I grew up, I think I had to get it this way. I was ever the artist and writer first.

5. Prothero and Williams, *Gaining a Face: the Romanticism of C.S. Lewis.*

6. Lewis, *Selected Literary Essays*, 265.

My imagination had to be set afire before my reason could even be interested in the claims of Christ.

Even today, I know many people who would deny being Christian with energy and conviction. But they would fall over themselves telling you how much they loved Aslan and Narnia. They are far more Christian than they know.

Nine: The Long Road Back

> It is good to have an end to journey toward; but it is the journey that matters, in the end.
>
> —*Left Hand of Darkness*, Ursula LeGuinn

So as I sat in the bedroom with *Surprised by Joy* in my hands, my jaw probably hanging open in stunned silence, and my heart on fire, having capitulated to Christ, the road stretched out before me. But my cure had only just begun. It is probably only a slight exaggeration to say I was a recovering joyaholic. Lewis is always quick to point out that mountaintop spiritual experiences are often followed by vast let-downs. I was no exception. I began to attend my parents' church, San Clemente Presbyterian, which was a good home to me for some years. I fell in with the youth group there and found an outlet for my bass and guitar skills. I even got to go on a choir tour as the guitarist to Seattle and back. I also found a new romance which gave me great happiness for a while. Ultimately though, there wasn't enough compatibility with her either; she recognized it before I did and ended it.

Actually, the high point at San Clemente Presbyterian was the brief but deep friendship with a young man just barely out of high school. Bryce Mittlestadt was a free-spirit, a hippie born too late, a blonde, blue-eyed connoisseur of laughter and freedom of spirit. He also played guitar and liked my kind of music. We briefly formed a duo, "Windriver," which though we only got one gig, was one of the best bands I played in. Sadly, he moved off to northern California and I saw little of him thereafter. Bryce always lived in the moment and hanging onto to distant friendships wasn't his strong suit. What he did for me in a larger sense was to disperse the last of my shyness and introversion. Bryce was fearless and made me realize, especially with people, that one need not care in the slightest what other people thought. The result was freedom and I'm grateful to him to this day.

More to the point, during my stay at San Clemente Presbyterian, I found good friends, but I found myself stumbling on the conservative Evangelical tendency to spurn thinking and settle for repeated patterns of thought that have been done for them. Though the church was nominally Presbyterian, it's members were primarily Evangelical and the theology was far more Baptist in some ways than Presbyterian. I remember one class I attended on a Sunday Morning on Bunyan's *Pilgrim's Progress* in which the only substantial insight was that the book was an allegory. The rest of the class we wrestled with tough questions like the "burden of sin" on Pilgrim's back, what could it symbolize? Sin? Brilliant. We took half an hour to figure that out. Again, I don't believe all of Christianity is divided between intellectual and stupid and that binary division itself is a fallacy created by sloth. After 32 years in the public schools, I believe people don't like to think and don't want to think. It's hard work. So the class was watered down to the point everyone was comfortable. If such a thing were done in the public schools where I work, there would be a firestorm of protest. I'm expected to push my students to the best of their mental abilities and I wouldn't be happy doing anything less. Somehow, in many churches, it's ok for Christians not to have to think, or even more, they think whatever they're taught. This alone is a vast turn off to millennials who increasingly see Christianity as the religion of brain-dead conformity. They never met Mr. M, but they fear him.

I sometimes wonder how much the Puritan heritage in American thought is responsible for our anti-intellectualism. Certainly the Puritans had a narrative of their own and suspected any ideas outside it. However, this pattern has migrated all over the country. One of my most conservative friends laments about how in his experience there is so little respect for deep and responsible thinking among the young people he teaches. He points out that

Christ expects the Christian to use all their mind, to be "as cunning as serpents and innocent as doves."[1]

About two years after my bedroom capitulation to Christ, I was working a job I didn't like. I was never cut out to be a bank teller and found it out fast. My San Clemente girlfriend was gone. The dull weight of Evangelical mental complacency was beginning to weigh both on me and my younger brother, John. About this time, Bruce Thielemann came out to California for a visit and preached at a Presbyterian church not too far up the road from us, where one of his proteges was pastor. We went to see Bruce, of course, and found ourselves very comfortable with the new Pastor, John Todd. Thus the stage was set.

A friend I had known at NAU was setting out for a backpack trip around Mt. Rainier in Washington State, on the Wonderland Trail. My restlessness was roaring. My heart was still sore from the loss of my San Clemente girlfriend, and heartbreak always made me restless. I quit my bank job, dumped the apartment I'd been living in, loaded the car with backpack gear and rambled on up to join him in Spokane. I'd known him at NAU since the post-Bob days and I think I made the mistake of thinking he could be another best buddy. But we never really clicked over the years, though we tried. On this backpack trip to Rainier, this dysfunction in our friendship came out glaringly. He approached backpacking with a competitive, driving intensity. I just wanted to wander through the woods. Years later, he ceased to return my calls and I lost track of him. It seems to me funny now how some friendships can end like divorces. And it brought home to me that to have even one true best friend is an incalculable gift. They are rare.

But more than this, as I destroyed my feet in badly fitting boots and we pushed our way around the mountain, not only did I realize that this friend and I couldn't really come to a meeting of the minds, but that here I was chasing joy again and I knew better. Living to just "experience life" in the hungry way I was going about it was self-defeating. Lewis had taught me that the achings of joy were really the desire to find Christ, and I had found this to be true.

1. Matt 10:16

Yet here I was again searching the mountains and woods for what I already had in my church. This is not to put down backpacking and hiking. My knees won't support a backpack anymore, but I still love to wander the woods. Yet I know that what the woods give me is a relatively small happiness. They are wonderful so long as I don't expect them to give me the meaning of the universe. The beauty of nature is a sign pointing beyond itself—not the point of arrival that we hunger for. Wordsworth misunderstood this in his early days, though it's a good thing he did, for much of his best poetry was about working through this misunderstanding.

When I arrived back at my parents' home, I had a quiet think for at least three days. I put it all together, in the same back bedroom in my folks' house where I'd capitulated to Christ. Here again I capitulated for a second time, and surrendered the fruitless rambling for joy. I would make something of my life at age 26. I would work. I would find a career. I would write. I would finally cease my denial and believe my Dad when he said if you want to live somewhere, you have to get a job there. I was even beginning to listen to those people around me who said I had a gift for teaching. Even now I believe that this moment of conversion—and the life of a Christian is filled with many moments of conversion—was far more significant than my first one with the Lewis book in my hand. That is why I believe it took me seven years, not five, to fully find faith again.

If the anti-intellectual atmosphere at San Clemente Presbyterian had a good effect on me, it was that it drove me to look for a Christianity that allowed for the full play of the mind and the heart, not just the heart. This time, the search was not hard. Bruce had already shown the way in guest preaching at the church of John Todd. My brother John, who was feeling much like I was, and I went there, to Geneva Presbyterian Church in Laguna Woods, California. John Todd's sermons fed my heart and mind the way Bruce Thielemann's had, though no one ever matched Bruce in sheer oratorical power. I stayed in that church till John Todd left it.

Also, now that I was listening, clues and open doors started coming at me. I took a job as a teacher's aide in a third grade class taught by a friend of my mom's. After some time, I found I was good at it and decided I might as well get an elementary credential and get paid the full salary for what I was doing. My first attempt at getting an elementary bilingual teaching job floundered. While I was in Spanish language school in Cuernavaca, Mexico, I heard about a junior high school in Long Beach hiring elementary school teachers to teach reading and English. Oddly, this is the job I ended up with for two years. It set me on the road to teaching high school English and I kept going down that road. I could have done elementary, but high school was my true niche. And I found it "accidentally"—but then Lewis tells us that for the Christian there are no coincidences.

Other pieces fell into place. One friend I made in a very unlikely way became important. I met John Monk in San Clemente when I was an NAU student visiting my folks. He worked at a gas station his dad owned. John was perhaps the friendliest person I'd ever known. We got to talking every time I came in to buy gas, and after a while we started to hang out together. He was in college as an English major, like me. He had a vintage Mustang, like me. It got so that when I was in San Clemente, I was hanging out with John, and it was always a good time. Now that I was back and trying to make something of my life, it was John who often led the way. He originally got me the environmental education jobs. (Heck, he may have got me all my significant jobs.) He encouraged me to think of teaching, which was what he was doing. About John, I want to say one other thing: John was and is a devout atheist. And yet we've always got along well. I think though we came to far different conclusions about faith, we had and have one thing in common, a very major thing. That is, we both believe what we believe because we believe it to be true, not convenient, not comforting, not popular, but true. We both insist on that rock-bottom integrity of faith or dis-faith. I highly recommend it.

It is odd, but as I said, many of the good jobs I have I got because John Monk knew somebody who was hiring. My junior high was a badly run school in a tough, urban neighborhood, so I quit it to try for grad school and a different kind of teaching. I had been at California State University at Fullerton for my credential and had taken a few English lit classes for the interest. I somehow wangled my way into the Masters in English program at Fullerton. I felt that I'd had about all of secondary teaching I was willing to take. I would be a full-time English professor at a four-year college. But I was learning that God has a tremendous sense of humor and despite the plans we make for our lives, he has his own ideas.

I was well into my first grad school classes when an opening showed up at Saddleback High School in south Santa Ana, California. For any who don't know, Santa Ana lies right in the middle of the conservative, white "OC", as Orange County is often called. But Santa Ana is a vast Mexican enclave. So a teacher there told her girlfriend about the opening. That girlfriend happened to be John Monk's girlfriend at the time. So she told John. John told me. I had finally realized my Dad was right, and though I really wanted to focus on grad school and college teaching, I interviewed. The principal, Nancy O'Connor, spent much of the interview asking me about my love for Dickens. She had been the English department chair. I was entirely at ease and not a speck nervous, mainly because I didn't really want the job. So, naturally, I got it. I told myself I'd do it for a year or two. God had other plans.

Ten: Anglicanism and What I Could Not Be

> He who begins by loving Christianity better than Truth will proceed by loving his own sect of church better than Christianity, and end by loving himself better than all.
>
> —*Aids to Reflection*, Samuel Taylor Coleridge

Before I go into Santa Ana and all that happened to me there, I need to catch up the stream of faith. I was happy with John Todd at Geneva Presbyterian. Still, I was very drawn to the Anglican balance of Lewis' thought and Bob, my best friend, had returned to his faith also. And he was an Anglican. I visited some Episcopal churches, as the Anglican Communion is called here in the US, and was impressed. But I couldn't leave John Todd. Suddenly, John Todd was getting divorced and half the congregation at Geneva was scandalized. Rather than cause a civil war in the church, John Todd found another church up in Malibu. It was 1984 and I moved to St Clement's by the Sea Episcopal Church in San Clemente.

Anglicanism turned out to be better than I could have dreamed up. It was balanced between Catholic and Protestant, both in thought and in its liturgy. It was and is a mix of warmth and dignity. It had what one writer called the "three-legged stool." That is, that Anglicans believed in Scripture-Tradition-Reason. There was no mindless obedience to dogma nor vacuous belief in anything that one felt like. It was a place for Christians whether smart or not, who were thinking Christians, and who wanted to believe what science had discovered without undergoing a crisis of faith. Granted, even in the Episcopal Church in America, there were conservatives and liberals. Anglicanism excludes nobody, so there's always the fringe, right and left. But in between, there was a home for all those Christians who didn't believe that using your mind is a sin and that dogma defined you as a Christian. Anglicans were and still are a small group in the US. But then, they always were. I have come to realize that size and purity in Christianity don't often go together. Usually, when the church gets large, that's also when it gets insincere and corrupt. Thus when someone brags to me how big their megachurch is, I'm dismayed rather than impressed.

There was much else about Anglicanism that I liked:

1. Holy calisthenics

Growing up Presbyterian, we were either sitting or standing. We listened to a sermon most of the time in church. Granted, if that were a Thielemann sermon, it could be a real rocket ride. If not, it could be a crashing bore. You sit there, and you listen, and you process. That's it. But having taken the best from the Catholic tradition, Anglicans cross themselves, stand, sit, and kneel. Like their Eastern Orthodox and Catholic brothers and sisters, Anglicans acknowledge that we humans don't just worship God with our minds, but with our bodies as well.

2. No church police

Really. No kidding. You want to kneel here and your neighbor feels compelled to stand there? Go for it. I'm not your judge. You generally won't get any strange looks for being out of step.

3. Focus on communion without the debate

Communion is every Sunday because Christ is in it and he is the center of everything. You are welcome to take that communion. I could spend a hundred pages trying to lay out the way the different Christian communions view the bread and the wine as Christ. Wars have been fought over this point and blood shed. The Anglican take?: It's Christ. We don't know how. Get over it. As Lewis said, "Here is big medicine and strong magic . . . the command, after all, was Take, eat: not Take, understand."[1]

4. Communion for all

You go into an Anglican church and you are told that if you seek Christ, you are welcome. Communion is not a litmus test reward. If you approach it wrongly, that's between you and God. You'll have to discuss that with him.

5. The BCP

The Book of Common Prayer, the Anglican center point and missal, is such fine spiritual poetry. As a poet, painter, and musician myself, I believe that good art aids worship. This is just darn good poetry. It's so good that half the people in this country would recognize the words to the wedding and funeral services without help. Behind the *King James Bible*, the *Book of Common Prayer* is the most widely known spiritual prose in the English language.

6. Women in the clergy

Episcopalians realized what I had long ago. Philogynist that I was, I could clearly see that God freely gave all the gifts of intelligence and social skill equally to women and men. Why could not women be clergy? And they are. And it works really rather well.

This is not to say that Anglicanism was always this way. They did their share of persecuting and being the state church where the cultural Christians made their bored obeisance to God for a begrudged hour a week. But something about the founding, where

1. Lewis, *Letters to Malcolm, Chiefly on Prayer*, 104.

Queen Elizabeth formed the early Anglican Church into a balance between Catholic and Protestant set a tradition of balance going that has survived the embarrassing missteps and thrived into today. And perhaps that was the best reason that I loved it—balance. The Anglican Church today may have its mix of liberals and conservatives and what I take to be a whole lot of people in between. But that's its beauty.

And the theme of my life carried through to here; just as I could never be a true liberal or true conservative in the theological world, I could not in the rest of the world.

I could never be a true conservative in the current sense of the word, because I feel I can't do that and be a Christian too. Some of the most important conservative assumptions today are the primacy of individualism, personal responsibility, and freedom from the restraints and demands of community as reflected in government. My libertarian friends hold all these sacred and and would go to the wall to fight for them. I cannot join them. I judge it to be important to balance individual needs with the need of community. If you follow Jesus you can't overlook the parable of the Good Samaritan. We *are* our brother's keeper, like it or not. And the government is the mechanism by which we do it as a nation. Ok, I can't prove this nor can you disprove it. We can all argue till we're blue in the face and many Americans do. I do however wonder if those of us who oppose using government as our mutual tool to even the playing field and somewhat offset the ravages of poverty and economic inequality, are really putting the Gospel first or their libertarian belief in personal responsibility. I do not know. That's between God and them. But for myself, I cannot ignore the demands of the Gospel.

But neither could I ever be a true liberal in the current sense of the word, because I find that current liberals, for all their open-mindedness, have their own orthodoxies that I question. I find so-called "postmodern" attitudes to be ridiculous (how can it be true that there are no truths?) and that relativism is merely an academic concept that no one actually attempts to live out. Try and tell anyone that the Holocaust was "relatively" acceptable. And like Lewis,

I'm not a pacifist. The world is a dangerous place and sadly we must do much to defend ourselves. Human nature is not so good that good will and diplomacy will solve all our conflicts.

I could go on about both pre-packaged philosophies but I think you get the idea. I can't be either; I'm a marshwiggle like Lewis. Not buying in to the pre-packaged binary imperative either conservative or liberal is a bit lonely and a little scary. Still, I recommend it.

Eleven: Love Vindicated and Watercolor Paint

> If you hear a voice within you say 'you cannot paint,' then by all means paint, and that voice will be silenced.
>
> —Vincent Van Gogh

The middle 80s years were a gift to me. Through Jim Thorburn, my friendship with Nigel rekindled. Nigel was my oldest friend outside of my family and though his rebellious rock 'n roller stage in high school parted us, once in adulthood, our old camaraderie resumed easily. I roomed with him for a time as well as with John Monk. Both men are dear to me to this day.

But the biggest splash came as a result of attending St Clement's. I remember seeing a young woman confirmed and baptized one Sunday. Her name was Gail Marie Fisher. She had long dark hair, pretty eyes, and was short, slender, and athletic. At a rectory party I met her. When I told the assistant rector, Fr. Rory, that Dickens' *David Copperfield* was my favorite novel, she standing there listening, decided I was something of a decent human being. Eventually I asked her out. Our first date was a hike. I cannot now remember all the sequence of dates. This was the fall of 1986 and I had just taken up my one or two year job at Saddleback High School and my work on my MA at Fullerton. But in Gail I found the deep companionship that I had only found once before with my lost NAU girlfriend. Though Gail was not a visual artist, she loved literature like I did and was as well-read as any college English major. Jane Austen was her passion and she had read every word

Jane ever wrote. She probably could have passed a stiff graduate exam in Austen. Gail shared my Anglican faith. Gail came from a gentle and loving family, much like mine, from Colorado farm stock, and had their nature. And Gail loved the outdoors and hiking like I did. She had devoted herself and her career to politics, but her issue was environmentalism. As a former environmental educator, I found I was in deep harmony with her on so many fronts. We met in September or maybe October. Unlike my other romances that foundered on incompatibility or insecurity, this one went smoothly. By the end of the following April of 1987 we were married in St Clement's by the Sea Episcopal Church.

And at this point, now that I've passed the moment hiking around Mt. Rainier where I woke up, I am going to abandon telling the stream of events in great detail. When one is on a journey, every stone is part of the story. Having arrived home is a very different kind of journey and everyday events, though subtly profound, provide little narrative insight. The year was 1987. I was at home in my faith, my career, my church, and now in my marriage. For Jane Austen, that would have been the place to end the novel. But God is the novelist that writes our lives, and we are the characters. Hereafter, change came to me in waves, not moments. The airplane has reached altitude and is cruising over long expanses. There won't be as many dips and climbs. There will only be small shifts in course.

And the most profound shift in my life came next. In 1989, I became father to a daughter, Sarah Marie. She was a quiet little girl with deep brown hair and big brown eyes, and she quickly inherited our love for art and reading. My parents fell head over heals in love with her. For though on a teacher's salary I could never afford much house, Sarah had access to my father's vast back yard for her own Narnia to explore and play in. Plus, she would camp out in my father's art studio while he made her castles and worlds with illustration board and his artistic genius. Or sometimes, my mother, who was so gifted in crafts that she probably was really a sculptor, would do paper mache or other paper projects fully including Sarah. It was my joy to see my daughter grow in such a world.

And the growth of my daughter re-awoke something long sleeping in me. We loved to go down to the public library, and Sarah would check out her limit of picture books. Plus, I was not shy in buying books for her. The art was beautiful and though I hadn't painted in over ten years, I picked up painting again, specifically watercolor. All that sleeping side of me woke up and I knew that I had to give it as much heart as I gave my writing. By the mid 2000s I had enough good paintings to put up a website and begin to look for galleries. As my practice grew, in time I dreamed of honoring my father's gift by becoming a successful painter in my own right.

But having a lovely wife and daughter clamped a restriction on one of my own dreams. I was still determined to leave secondary behind and move on to full time college teaching. I finished my MA in English two months after Sarah was born and applied for community college work, getting part time at Orange Coast College in Costa Mesa. But doctoral work seemed impossible without going into poverty as a TA at some university, something neither Gail nor I were willing to do. I applied for and got in the Master of Fine Arts program in creative writing at Chapman University, hoping this would open up doors. Yet, more and more, the high school teaching job that I thought was a two-year temporary, became my mainstay. Life was not going according to my plan. And I had learned that just restlessly throwing over a job as I had often done in the past, was no solution. And it wasn't' possible with a wife, daughter and mortgage. I hoped I would write a best-selling novel that would free me from the grind of teaching high school. Plus, my good principals left and a series of horrible principals followed. The job became obnoxious. I wanted out desperately. The old "Jackson Browne" me would have bolted. Instead, I hunkered down for my family and did everything I could to get a full time college job. Those were my plans. God had other plans.

Twelve: There's No Place Like Rome

> For Christ plays in ten thousand places,
> Lovely in limbs, and lovely in eyes not his
> To the Father through the features of men's faces.
>
> —Gerard Manley Hopkins

During these years, my discovery of the Southern California C.S. Lewis Society was a godsend—and that quite literally. I met well-read and intelligent Christians. Some were conservative, some liberal. Some were Evangelical, but many were Catholic. Ultimately they were all "mere Christians" as Lewis would have said. I became the editor of the journal, *The Lamp Post,* which was the premier Lewis journal on the west coast through the 90s when I was editor. This allowed me to meet all sorts of people. I became friends with Walter Hooper, Lewis' secretary, and Doug Gresham, one of his step-sons.

There I met Paul Ford, the Catholic theologian and prominent Lewis scholar. He deepened and enlarged my understanding of Lewis in ways for which I am still profoundly grateful. Summer workshops were held at a Benedictine monastery in the high desert north of Los Angeles, St Andrew's Abbey. Beyond its Lewis connection, the abbey itself became a place of spiritual retreat for me and I eventually became an oblate, third order Benedictine. It also went a long way toward undoing all the anti-Catholic prejudices I'd been taught as a boy. My Irish Catholic grandfather had divorced my grandmother, and my mother had sided with her mother and blamed the Catholic Church in part. I was reading much on ancient church history at this time and finding out all the subtle and complicated truths about the founding of the Catholic, Orthodox, and Protestant positions. I knew from my reading alone that much of the debate between Christian sects turned on theological positions that in many cases had become obsolete over the centuries.

However, about this time a new rector came to St Clement's who was a true far-left liberal. I didn't get much feeding from a pastor who thought much of the Nicene Creed was metaphorical. My wife wanted to try out the Catholic Church, so we began to attend Mission San Juan Capistrano about the time Sarah was born. I look back on this now as a lover's quarrel I was having with the Episcopal church. It lasted all through the nineties and well into the 2000s, when I returned to St Clement's a surely as a homing pigeon.

But I have no regrets about my time in Rome. It was at very least, a marvelous education. And I learned that much of what I'd been taught about the Catholic Church was misunderstood or just plain wrong. All those variations on "The Catholic Church teaches you have to earn your way to Heaven by good works and rituals" (Pelagianism) were the misperceptions of marginally educated ex-Catholics. There are some popular devotions (like certain novenas), that are explained in terms of "say this prayer nine times and God will give you what you want," that probably should have been disciplined by the Church. But what the Church itself actually taught was the Christian paradox of faith and works that every Christian denomination wrestles with—essentially the content of the book of James in the New Testament. But there were things that were different and even refreshingly different about the Catholic Church. I'll list a few:

1. Every church was a branch office. When I was Protestant, I knew of lots of churches who felt that they were the ONLY church in the world that had the faith down correctly. The minute details of dogma were the password to salvation or failing them, a road to damnation. The Catholic Church really is "catholic", that is universal. There are a billion little

Protestant churches out there, eyeing each other suspiciously, but one Catholic Church with branch offices everywhere. I know I am suspicious of large churches—the Catholic Church is far and away the largest body of Christians on the planet—but the local branch organization did much to allay that. You could be a Catholic welcome at mass on seven continents and yet well known to your local parish priest in your tiny local parish.

2. Once I was a practicing Catholic, I ceased to worry about whether I knew who was and who wasn't saved. As a Catholic, I knew that only God knows the hearts of people, and though I might feel awfully sure about someone, ultimately only God knew. This was so liberating. I had always felt the burden of the Calvinistic obsession with who was the elect and who not. Now I merely shrugged and said, "God knows!"

3. I cannot possibly express how liberating it was to take my weight off the Bible. What I mean is that all my life as a Protestant, everything turned on how the Bible was, or was not minutely to be interpreted. We "stood on the Bible," and sometimes I think of it metaphorically as tipping this way and that, as Protestants battled each other over interpretation, like a brawl raging on a small, pitching boat at sea. As a Catholic, the Bible was but one part of tradition. The sense of the Church overall was far more important. This was freedom.

4. The Church was mystical. All my Native American studies had given me a taste for the mystic. Every mass is mystical, the mystery of the death and life of Christ re-enacted, outside time, inside time, happening now and always. The sacredness of the bread and the wine made so much sense to me.

5. "Invincible Ignorance": I know it sounds like an insult, but it was really vastly liberating. Though the Catholic Church still holds that it is the original Church and all others are "in schism", that is, split-offs, since Vatican 2, the church has taught that those whose experiences or lack of exposure to

> the Gospel keep them from believing, are not condemned. They have no real fair exposure to the Gospel and God will not condemn them for that. That could mean the person with psychological or personal problems, or weird misunderstandings is not going to be turned away. If their ignorance of the Gospel can't be conquered (which is what "invincible" means) because of circumstances, it won't be held against them. This entirely does away with the Fundamentalist picture of anyone not going through a public altar call conversion being swept screaming into Hell. God's going to save a lot more people than we imagine and from times and places we wouldn't have suspected. This goes back to not knowing who is saved.

All in all, my years in the Catholic Church were wonderful. I was in the band for the 9 o'clock mass for some years, my longest band gig ever. So why did I leave it again? Well, all that time, I still missed the Episcopal form of worship. My parish was actually what I'd call Evangelical-Catholic, and so very conservative unlike many Catholic parishes, that it was the one parish George W. Bush chose to visit when he was running for president and needed to shore up Catholic support. My daughter was in the school there, but after she left and my band broke up, I felt less connected. I tried two other parishes. But deep down I had never believed the Catholic assertion that they were the One True Church. I had always believed Rome was a significant part of the Church, maybe even the most significant, but still only a part.

Two things said by friends, inadvertently in both cases, caused me to think. A friend of mine at Lewis Society said, "Did you go to Rome to escape the problems in the Episcopal Church?" Well, in hindsight, yes, I had. But Rome has its own problems, and its own super-conservatives and super-liberals. Then Bob said, referring entirely to himself and with no intention of influencing me, "I could never be Catholic because I don't believe all they teach." I had to think about that. I didn't either. As much as I loved the Roman church, I found that their claim to inspiration was questionable, and that I couldn't accept their whole teaching on birth control and sexuality, nor the whole theology of Purgatory as it exists in the catechism.

In the end, when I felt it was time to move parishes, I opened my mind to both Catholic and Anglican parishes as options. I eventually found myself back home at St Clements, which had a new and wonderful rector. To my mind I haven't left the Catholic Church; I've just moved laterally in it. I still love to go to masses. And if the Anglican option weren't available to me, I'd join a Catholic parish in a heartbeat. But I know I can't wave the Catholic catechism and say I buy it all.

I, like Lewis, am a Mere Christian.

Lewis was careful not to define it much other than to say it was what all Christians now believe. Probably the Nicene Creed and not much more define it. Part of my comfort in the Anglican Communion is that these sorts of things are not restrained by any catechism—one is allowed to follow one's conscience. But all this took place in the context of my Jacobian wrestle with God—over my job.

Thirteen: Santa Ana and PhD

> Understanding comes with life. As a man grows he sees life and death, he is happy and sad, he works, plays, meets people—sometimes it takes a lifetime to acquire understanding, because in the end understanding simply means having sympathy for people.
>
> —*Bless Me, Ultima* by Rudolfo Anaya

I was desperate through the mid nineties to dump my high school job and go to full time college. I applied many places. I finished the second masters in creative writing at lovely little Chapman University under an excellent novelist and writing instructor, Gordon McAlpine. I looked for PhD programs that I could do. Meanwhile, at work I had lousy principals and was often dealing with students struggling with both skills and behavior problems. It wasn't much fun.

By the late 90s, I had a new hope. I was accepted on a part time basis that allowed me to continue supporting my family, into a doctoral program in British literature at the University of Wales. That was a wonderful experience, but it took forever, and by the time I had degree in hand, I was in late middle age. The reality was that there were and are very few college jobs and a hoard of younger people trying out for them. And the four-year jobs in English mostly go to graduates from Harvard, Yale, and Berkeley. The odds were heavily stacked against me.

And looking back now, I realize this was a huge test for me and my restlessness. All my life I had just bolted out the door when things got tough or ugly. Here I could not without failing my girls, my wife and daughter. I bucked up and took it. I didn't like it at the time. It didn't fit my plan for what I wanted for my life. Yet, each year while this was happening, many students let me know clearly that they had enjoyed my classes and that I was a favorite and influential teacher to them. It seems arrogant to talk about it, but I was able to connect to these young people time and again. Maybe it was because I had that witty Gregg Brown verbal patter full of irony and puns. Maybe it was because I refused to "talk down" to anyone and they felt I treated them with respect. Maybe it was because I always sensed when they were confused and went back and explained things again and again without rancor or making them feel stupid for asking. I don't know. These things were high expectations I had of myself in front of a classroom. But every year there were more and more kids who wanted to sign my yearbook and have their picture taken with me. With the coming of Facebook, these grads would friend me and then share with me their lives in college, becoming spouses and parents.

One thing I never foresaw was that spending 30 or more years in a Mexican enclave, I found myself unable to ever form that paranoid sort of white racism that sits in a gated community and builds dread and misunderstanding about people of color and people who speak something besides English. I learned to love and be a part of this Latino community, to pick up the cultural nuances and understand them. The best cure for prejudice is to actually get to know someone as a human being that you might be tempted to be prejudiced against. I think I did alright in opening my heart; I was privileged to be at two Mexican-style weddings. And I have to say these beautiful Mexican-American students changed me far more than I think I changed them. *Gracias, amigos.*

I remember it in three waves. The first wave was the late 80s and early 90s. I was a rookie and yet I had some great classes. The Class of 91 was especially memorable, with a score of kids that I still am in touch with today. One is my attorney. But when I started at Saddleback, it was like an Olympic village with over 19 languages on campus and every ethnic group imaginable. In the 90s, the good principals I had moved on and we had some questionable ones. Plus the district opened two magnet schools, pulling away our best students, diverted all special education students to us, then criticized us for letting our scores go down. It was a hard time for me.

The second wave was the late 90s and early 2000s. It was a better time for me though I had to endure another horrible principal. But I saw how many of these now majority Latino students struggled with language and education to the point where many of them just gave up and dropped out, or maybe they just passively did as little as possible. It would have been easy to do what so many people of my race have done and assume they were all lazy. But that wasn't very rational. A few here and there, sure, but large swaths of them? As the years went on and I read student papers, I realized that even the successful students were struggling against huge odds at home and at school. Many had home environments where study was impossible. Most had parents who were nearly or fully illiterate in both English and Spanish. There was no help for homework. I saw first hand how poverty retards educational progress.

Around 2007 things got better and better. Still, students struggled and I struggled to do what I could to bridge the divide between what they knew coming in and what was expected of them. I really felt this when I taught Advanced Placement English Literature. I felt as if my students didn't start at the starting line with that class—they started 40 yards back of the starting line. I understood and yet agonized when so many kids just gave up and shuffled their way through on minimum effort.

But their hearts were ever open and I've known more kindness there than anywhere. I really learned the truth of the claim that the poor are more generous than the wealthy, even when they have nothing much to give. It took me years to realize that this tough road was the one I needed to take.

I still struggled in my mind with why, after all I'd done to prepare for a full time college career, God had kept the door closed to leaving Saddleback High School. Why God? But God didn't answer quickly. Like I said, he is not impressed by our impatience. And I had plenty of impatience for him to not be impressed by. As better principals and better days returned to Saddleback High in the 2000s, I found that instead of the struggling rookie teacher or middle of the pack workhorse teacher, I was becoming an honored veteran. Me? Honored? It was astounding to me. I was appointed English Department co-chair and found a new interest in helping my department members with their problems and challenges. I learned to grow, survive, and thrive in spite of a decade or more of adversity. The restless me would have never stayed the course. But God seemed to have boxed me in and forced me through painful growth, growth I would never have had as a full time college teacher.

About the same time, my elder brother Don was having tremendous difficulties in his full time college job over the politics in his geology department. I knew other college level academics with the same problem. College profs seemed to love to make war on each other. And I learned that there was something like a 600 to 1 ratio of jobs to qualified graduates in college full time teaching. I was dreaming of entering a career field that was highly impacted and nearly impossible to penetrate. Meanwhile, I had taught successfully in part time college, first at Orange Coast College and later at Santa Ana College for almost as many years as I had at Saddleback. I began to realize I had in fact been given what I'd asked for, but it didn't look like what I wanted. I *was* a college prof—just part time. But it was better in the end than what I wanted. God loves us so much that he often gives us, not what we ask for, not what we think we want, but what we really need. It is a hard thing to see. It's part of what Lewis called the "intolerable compliment."

As for my Jacobian wrestle with God, wouldn't you know it—he pinned me.

Fourteen: Christ and the Millennial

> I have no faith in human perfectibility. I think that human exertion will have no appreciable effect upon humanity. Man is now only more active—not more happy—nor more wise, than he was 6000 years ago.
>
> —Edgar Allan Poe

So that is my story. Yet, what can I say to my daughter's generation? Will any of this be meaningful? After all, my history took place in a world very different from yours, as I'm sure you noticed if you read the previous chapters. How is any of that relevant? Well, yes, technology and the way we look at technology has changed a lot. The human heart never changes. I tell my students that they are just as noble, brave, intelligent, but also as greedy, stupid and selfish as their ancestors. You inherit human nature the same as your forebears even if you do play Pokemon Go on your phone. As a generation, you live in a world of technology, suspended on a platform of digital devices and internet access as surely detached from the earth as George Jetson. Your myths feature zombies and vampires. Both are symbols of darkness which make me believe you are not optimistic. In fearing zombies, you are fearing a loss of your living humanity, and that it may be taken from you by sub-humans teaming about you and threatening to drag you in. It's pretty much the same fear that we all had when we saw the body-snatcher movies. In fearing, or perhaps envying vampires, you recognize that survival in this world seems to entail taking ruthless advantage of others, feeding on them. The vampire is a perfect metaphorical picture of the sharp business man. You have very mixed feelings about this. But there again, you recognize that this is a loss of a part of your humanity. That's why Edward in the *Twilight* series is at one time attractive and repelling. He is moral, and doesn't feed on humans, yet, he too is a deathless sub-human fragment.

The world around you is often a dark and confusing place. You do not share the post World War 2 optimism of your grandparents at all. You see yourselves like Harry Potter, using limited good magic to fight the death-eaters and Voldemort. And why, for God's sake, in such a world, would you want to become a Christian? Wouldn't that mean becoming a conservative? Aren't they the same thing? Isn't Christianity just a bunch of rules? What about other religions? How can one be right and all the others wrong? I can't believe a good God would throw people into Hell.

I'll address these one at a time.

1. Why be a Christian? I'd say *don't* be a Christian unless you can't help yourself. Here I would go back to Lewis—remember, a glass of port is more likely to make you happy. There is really only one good reason to become a Christian: you really, *really,* honestly and truly can't help but think that the carpenter from Nazareth was God visiting humanity. Sure, people have other reasons, but those reasons tend to fade or be absorbed in some other cause. GK Chesterton wrote that Christianity had not been tried and failed; Christianity had been tried, found hard, and given up. If you really think that Jesus of Nazareth was God, then you have to try to follow what he taught, and that is hard, very hard. If you think I'm kidding, just go ahead and try to live the Sermon on the Mount for one week. Be my guest. Good luck with that. Sure, it's easy to call yourself Christian, cherry-pick the Gospel for the parts that make you comfortable, and show up to church now and then. Most people who call themselves Christians in this country do exactly that. But if that's your idea of Christianity, you are fooling yourself. Christ himself told people to "count the cost." Don't do this unless you really want to sign up for the whole treatment. The up side is that you'll have stepped into the True Light. It's dangerous and it can be painful. It's a bit like joining Dumbledore's

Army in the face of powerful opposition. Don't do it unless you're willing to pay the price.

2. Do I have to become a conservative too? Sadly, across history there has been a lot of what Lewis called "Christianity and," that is people who strap the Gospel to their cause to give it legitimacy. As Lewis pointed out this invariably ends up with a) Christianity becoming a mere sticker on the body of some other movement, and b) Christianity being discredited for the sins of that movement. As I discussed in previous chapters, this began happening in America back in the 60s and now there are many who call themselves Christian who equate that faith with being a Republican conservative. I was repelled by Mr. M. Only God knows what his faith really amounted to, or anyone like him. And I've known many conservatives, mainly through my Lewis connections, who are passionate about following Christ. The world is not black and white like in Harry Potter. Most of us are shades of gray. Or if it is like anything in Harry Potter, we are all like Prof Lupin, who, though a good and kind wizard, struggles against the werewolf raging inside him. I don't know what you or anybody has to go through with their own inner werewolves.

But though it doesn't get much press coverage, there are many churches in America that don't believe in that union of Christian and conservative at all. My Episcopal Church is one. Many of the so-called "mainline" churches don't either. And even many Evangelicals have rejected the marriage with conservatism. And while you're at it, don't let the strictness stories of Catholic schools, or the sad priest sexual scandals give you the wrong impression—the Catholic Church is still a home to nameless thousands doing the kind of work every day that Mother Teresa got famous for. It's no accident that Dorothy Day and the Catholic Worker movement came from that direction. It's a church proudly multi-racial and multi-cultural and with many people quietly doing Christ's work on earth. And if that weren't enough, the current pope, Francis, is no Pharisee.

Also, the magazine *Sojourners* is a rallying point for Christians who cannot equate their faith with conservatism and you can find that online. They believe Christ has called us to reject racism and serve each other. And here I should point out that many of the people at *Sojourners* are Evangelicals. So don't fall for the media generalization that all Evangelicals are conservatives. From there you can go many directions. And don't be put off by the fact that this non-conservative side of Christianity is small right now. Christianity at its best is always small.

Really, the far right would have you think that your choice is between your conscience and your faith, that conservative values *are* Christian values, and that to reject conservative values is to be "liberal Christian" who believes in nothing and has lost touch with the faith as given by the apostles. But the reality is there is a large Christian community, faithful to everything in the Nicene Creed, who don't believe that being conservative has anything to do with Jesus Christ.

3. Isn't Christianity just a bunch of rules? Another sad fact, or perhaps reality of history is that most movements of any kind start in inspiration and end up being codified into a set of rules. This happened in even Jesus' time with the Pharisees, so that we now call having a lot of picky rules "pharisaism." You may remember how much respect Jesus gave the Pharisees' rules. It got him killed. Of course it's possible to go off the deep end in the other direction and not really believe anything other than having good spiritual feelings. People these days do a lot of both. There are still plenty of Pharisees around today; Mr. M was clearly one, and sadly there are plenty of people like Mr. M around today. Make no mistake though, for every Mr. M, there are many people who call themselves Evangelical and serve the poor and needy, not connecting their faith to conservative politics. The news media tends to talk in terms of large movements. The people actually doing Christ's work in the world tend not to advertise. Don't rely on stereotypes; look closely for yourself.

Christianity has been codified many ways by many churches. But George MacDonald, a writer who influenced Lewis, told us in effect, unless you know the mind of Christ and live that, the doctrines and dogmas are useless. Lewis stuck to only those doctrines all Christians believe, his "mere Christianity." I would say, don't focus on rules. Sure, you're going to come to believe some sort of specifics, but don't let defense of your understanding be more important than living out the Gospel as you find it in the New Testament. That know-it-all approach to theology sort of assumes that you can do this on your own. You can't. It's only by the grace of God can we do anything at all.

Close all those rule books, books of apologetics, and catechisms and open up your New Testament instead. Start with the Gospels and Christ's own teachings. Pray, and trust God to help you try to live up to that. That alone will take a you whole lifetime and you'll never finish. In fact, if you're like me, you'll botch it pretty badly. But God is forgiving and the only real unforgivable sin is not picking yourself up from the dust and trying again. And you won't need to consult anyone's rules either. Remember what St Paul says about love in the first book of Corinthians. If you can't do things out of love, you might as well not do them at all. It's about love, not rules.

4. What about other religions? How can one be right and all the others wrong? This one bothered me for a long time too. And Christianity in its early days attributed other religions to the devil. But it was also a block for Lewis, who was only able to believe Christianity when he came to believe that all religions have significant chunks of truth to them, and many of the pagan myths echo the story of Christ. Lewis came to believe that Christ was the fulfillment of the "good dreams" of paganism. On top of this, bearing in mind the Catholic concept of "invincible ignorance" and our own entire inability to judge whom God loves and whom he doesn't, I'd say the question actually burns down to something else. Lewis himself hinted in the Chronicles of Narnia to such a thing. He has a Calormene (the baddies) officer named "Emeth" go looking for his god Tash and instead he finds Aslan. Aslan explains that because Emeth was looking with an open heart and mind, he found the real God, even if he got the names confused. Lewis never went so far as to try and state this as a principal, but he felt that God is just, and all our honest searchings, if they're really honest, will be honored. Still, it was Aslan that Emeth found, not another god. So in Lewis' vision, truth is widespread across religions, but Christ is God visiting earth.

Still have a problem with that? Well, if you think about it, there are two things to pay attention to: a) there is tremendous similarity in what the major religions teach. Most of this I'd put down to Natural Law, but it is true. And this leads many people to say that all religions are one. That would be a lovely sentiment except, b) they have major disagreements. The big sticking point is the carpenter from Nazareth. He said "before Abraham was born I AM," (John 8:58) which was a claim to be the Hebrew god on earth. Mohammad thought Jesus to be only a prophet, and would have considered such a statement, if made in front of him, blasphemy. The Buddha would have considered the whole idea silly and irrelevant. A Hindu would wonder how that would fit in with the existing pantheon of gods, like Krishna. You can't have a flat tire and not have a flat tire. Christ can't have said this and not have said this. It's mainly what got him killed. It's not like it was some minor point in his teaching we can wave away. Those are the facts. Logically you can conclude a) they're *all* wrong, b) one of them is right and the others wrong, c) they're not wrong, but this Christ was a crazy dude or a liar. The trouble with C is how are his moral teachings are going to be worth anything if he was crazy or lying? And that was my first point of this little chapter: was Jesus Christ God like he claimed to be? If you think so, then other faiths may have much truth in them, but they missed this fact. If not, like St Paul says,

> . . . your faith is futile; you are still in your sins. Then those who have fallen asleep in Christ have perished. If our hope in Christ is for this life alone, we are to be pitied more than all men. . . . [1]

Or to put it in current language, if Christ isn't who he said he was and risen from the dead, we're screwed. I'm all for those devoted to religions respecting each others' faiths and peacefully

1. 1 Cor 15

co-existing. That's the way it should be. But none of that matters to the question of truth if Christ is a pleasant myth or a lie. If that's the case, you'd be nuts to be a Christian. Everything turns around how you react to this outrageous claim.

5. I *can't believe a good God would throw people into Hell.* Here Lewis was a great help to me. The reason so many people stumble on this is because preachers both Catholic and Protestant over the last five centuries or so have been trying to scare cultural Christians into a real commitment with stories of hellfire. As a pastoral technique it really doesn't work and it gives people strange ideas about Hell. The Middle Ages were rife with scare-art meant to frighten people into opening their hearts to God. About the only good thing that came out of that was the fantastic gargoyle art on Gothic cathedrals.

But imagine a man, call him Joe X. Joe X is a good church man, but unknown to his wife, he is getting rich on the side running sex-slaves from Asia. He crushes the dreams of hundreds of unsuspecting girls and forces them into prostitution, drugs and an eventual young death, all for his profit. He dies of a heart attack one day after giving a friend a long speech on how everyone is a sucker but him. So he faces God. Will he go to eternity to enjoy the presence of God and all the things that go with it? I'd say he'd hardly enjoy a reality where he couldn't sucker someone. All his life he's been his own god; do you really think he'll want to surrender that? If he does, there's hope. That's called repentance. So it's more than a matter of Joe X needing to repent. If he doesn't change his heart, how could he enjoy Heaven? (unless, of course, God lets him start a sex slave business up there . . . yeah, not likely). In short, we have to change to become the sort of people that would even want to live forever in the joy and presence of the creator.

And if Joe X won't repent what is there? This is why Lewis put it so well when he said that the doors to Hell were locked from the inside. We will all be given the choice and chance to surrender ourselves to joy and life and to live in the bright eternity of God. But if we'd rather keep our pride, our greed, our self-worship, our possessiveness, or just hunker down in our fears, God gives us free will. And that state of refusing joy is called Hell. And I've known people like that in this life, who work really hard at being miserable. For them, Hell has already started. I'm betting you know people like that too.

If this doctrine is scary to you, it should be for the right reason. It's not about that imagery of devils and flames. That's metaphor. It's about clutching onto things that we prefer to God, to being happy in his presence. What have we each to give up, to let go of? The Rich Young Ruler wouldn't let go of his money to follow Jesus. Are we any different? For me, I had to let go of my dream to be a full time college teacher and work my way through the good and the bad in the Mexican barrio. But thank God I did.

Fifteen: Recognition

> He asked her, "Woman, why are you crying? Who is it you are looking for?" Thinking he was the gardener, she said, "Sir, if you have carried him away, tell me where you have put him, and I will get him." Jesus said to her, "Mary." She turned toward him and cried out in Aramaic, "Rabboni!" (which means "Teacher").
>
> —John 20:15, 16

All that's very interesting you're sure, but then sure is what you're really not. How can you be *sure? How can anyone be sure about God, about eternity, about reality and the meaning of life?* People mean different things when they ask that question, so I have to address it's varying possible meanings. First, face it: it's such a *fantastic leap* to believe that one man, a first century Jew from a nowhere corner of Israel was the Creator of this vast cosmos visiting us. It's a claim that ET was actually a Jewish carpenter and not a small, cute creature in Spielberg's spaceship. How can anyone ask anyone to believe such a thing? My answer is: you're right. It's an incredible leap, an outrageous gamble, a long-shot crap-shoot.

And so is everything else.

I have friends and family who are devout atheists. They would jump up at this point and say it's a gamble not to be taken seriously. We should stick to what we can prove scientifically and actually know. Well, I won't go into the problem that raises with the self-defeating philosophy called "logical positivism." Ok, fine, but then what about their gamble? They are so sure that what we can measure and gauge is the universe and all the universe there is. If we can't somehow detect it, it's not there. This position has been called materialism, ie, the belief that only the material world exists. Pushed to it's full logical extreme it is logical positivism. But any honest physicist would laugh at the notion that all reality is detectable. Reality is constantly throwing up twists that defy what we've always known. Quantum physics have cast doubt on Einsteinian physics. And ultimately the notion that only that which we can measure and detect exists is a leap of faith in itself. The atheists are rolling the dice just like the rest of us.

I say this with no disrespect for what science can actually find. As I said in earlier chapters, I was raised to have a profound respect for science and the truth as it is discernible. But that's very different from saying that *all* truth is scientifically discernible. My favorite analogy for this is that God is a novelist and we are all characters. For him, time, gravity and space itself are his tools and toys. Once you realize the incredible nature of his caring about us on this mote of dust we call our home, dwarfed by a galaxy that is yet another mote of dust dwarfed by the universe, you will realize the un-graspable and vast scope of his love and humility. And you will realize that no instrument nor telescope of ours could ever "detect" and "measure" him anymore than Hamlet could detect Shakespeare, or Oliver Twist detect Dickens.

So the atheist is right beside me with his dice in his hand. Actually, the safest (if safety really comes into this at all) way is to be agnostic, to refuse to roll the dice at all. And though many people in this country would confuse agnosticism with atheism, they're not the same. Most people, the vast majority, in this country, though they wouldn't own the name, are in fact agnostic. Oh, sure, they'll tell you they're Christian, but they never really read the Bible, nor hardly darken the door of any church. And if you got them alone and they were really honest, they'd say they go to church on the rare occasions that they do because their mama told them decent people do (cultural Christianity again) and deep down they really don't know if they believe anything besides trying to make a living and hoping to win the lottery. Though they'd be reluctant to admit it, their whiff of cultural Christianity is pretty useless to them. And that's because cultural Christianity is in fact useless and misleading. They've just enough of a smidgen of science education from their youth to doubt the miraculous and be vague materialists, but just enough little shreds of faith left over from their raising to have a vague notion of God. More than anything, their energies are directed not to Christ, though they may attend church every once in a while, but to their own prosperity and what dreams they still cling to. It's a sad picture, but it's a picture of the vast majority of "Christian America." It's what Thoreau was thinking of when he said that "most men live lives of quiet desperation." And all of them in the final analysis, if they're not already so, would do almost anything to be rich, which means their real god is Prosperity. Jesus knew of this god. He called him "Mammon." I have long suspected that the real dominant religion in America is not Christianity, but the worship of the great god Prosperity.

Still, I prefer such people vastly to those who take some cruel extremism, political or otherwise, and pursue it in the name of Christ. "Of all bad men, religious bad men are the worst" Lewis tells us, and he's absolutely right.

These I've described above are muddy ways to roll the dice, sadly. But they are us. Ultimately, whether we opt for prosperity-worship, Buddhism, Hinduism, New Age beliefs, a vague nature-theism, atheism, Christianity, or whatever, you are rolling the dice. You can hold your dice and be agnostic, but that doesn't answer any questions.

I told you before that the only reason to be Christian is because you can't help it, you can't help but roll your dice for the Jewish carpenter from Nazareth. But why would you go and do a thing like that? Funny, but I want to say it's because you recognize him.

No, I'm not kidding.

You recognize him.

For me, once all the logical objections had been cleared, I knew him. I can't really explain it, but I knew and recognized him. And before you accuse me of coming out of theological la-la land, there is quite a bit of scriptural support for this. "My sheep know my voice; I know them and they follow me."[1] I've already quoted at the head of the chapter the scene in the Gospel of John where Mary Magdalene recognizes Jesus after the Resurrection. We have no reason other than the pictures of him as a handsome, bearded, white man from the Sunday School Jesus literature to think he was good looking or charming. He most likely was a rather plain-looking, dark-skinned, Galilean Jew, probably dressed simply, a country bumpkin to the eyes of the more sophisticated people around the capitol, Jerusalem. But many people recognized him. They followed him around and listened to him. This is why it's important that you read his actual words first and do not filter your understanding through someone else's agenda. When the religious authorities of the time sent men to arrest Jesus, they were so transfixed by his words they couldn't carry out their mission.[2] His words resonate out of dusty bibles over two millennia and grab people's hearts today. People recognize him. Even when he speaks of the judgment at the end of time, where many claim him and he turns them away, he does so with the words, "Then I will tell them plainly, 'I never knew you. Get away from me, you who practice evil!'"[3] Therefore we must conclude that the critical thing is not to subscribe to some list of "thou-shalt-nots" or any particular formula for behavior, Bible-belt rules or otherwise; the critical thing is to be known by him. And for that to happen, you must recognize him in all the fog, in all the shouting alternatives of religion and philosophy that compete for our attention and allegiance in this wide and varied world. And you have to walk toward him. He knows you. You recognize him. You follow him. The rest is frosting.

The book I cited before, Lewis's *The Last Battle,* is the Chronicle of Narnia that talks about the end of time and Christ and there are two scenes in it that are relevant here. The first is the one I mentioned before, where the young officer of the enemies of Narnia

1. John 10:27
2. John 7:46
3. Matt 7:23

(the Calormenes), by the name of Emeth, goes to Aslan's country seeking the god Tash, whom he has worshiped all his life. As he relates later, he finds Aslan instead. They talk. Emeth relates what happens next:

> ... I said, Alas Lord, I am no son of thine but the servant of Tash. He answered, Child, all the service thou hast done to Tash, I account as service done to me. Then by reasons of my great desire for wisdom and understanding, I overcame my fear and questioned the Glorious One and said, Lord, is it then true, as the Ape said, that thou and Tash are one? The Lion growled so that the earth shook (but his wrath was not against me) and said, It is false. Not because he and I are one, but because we are opposites, I take to me the services which thou hast done to him. For I and he are of such different kinds that no service which is vile can be done to me, and none which is not vile can be done to him. Therefore if any man swear by Tash and keep his oath for the oath's sake, it is by me that he has truly sworn, though he know it not, and it is I who reward him. And if any man do a cruelty in my name, then, though he says the name Aslan, it is Tash whom he serves and by Tash his deed is accepted. Dost thou understand, Child? I said, Lord, though knowest how much I understand. But I said also (for the truth constrained me), Yet I have been seeking Tash all my days. Beloved, said the Glorious One, unless thy desire had been for me thou wouldst not have sought so long and so truly. For all find what they truly seek.[4]

This is not to say that all religions are one. Aslan quite clearly dislikes the thought in the passage. It is to say that to pursue truth unflinchingly, wherever it appears, brings you closer to Christ. This is why both Lewis and I feel unthreatened by the existence of alternative faiths or even the sincere atheism of people like my friend, John. John pursues his atheism because he believes it to be true, and he loves the truth. I believe that people like that will recognize Aslan when the right time comes.

4. Lewis, *The Last Battle*, 156.

But it's also quite clear that what is essential is integrity. All find what they truly seek, but you have to truly seek. This is far more important that "Christianity conquering the world" as some seem to think God's intention is. This is not to say that doctrine is useless nor unimportant. But Christ says "By their fruits you will know them"[5] and his tale of the goats and sheep has to do with action, not doctrinal affiliation. American Protestantism is often fixated with fine doctrinal and theological points, and with separating from those who disagree. Christ nowhere in the New Testament seems to share this urge to separate from those without doctrinal purity. He is far more concerned with the need for clothes, mercy to lonely prisoners, and lonely sick people.[6]

The second image is from the same book later on where there is a large door opening onto Narnia and Aslan calls that world to a close. As darkness descends onto Narnia and all the creatures are drawn to the light of the door, they have one of two reactions: they either look at Aslan in loathing and fear and turn back to the darkness, or they look on him in love and enter his country. I am sure that Lewis made this passage as a piece of fantasy literature and not as some doctrine. But I believe the reality won't be far different.

We recognize him—or we don't. He knows us—or he doesn't. Not much else matters.

Some would question all I've said here and criticize it for being too reliant on the accuracy of the Bible, specifically the Gospels and Acts. That's a long and strident controversy. I have concluded, like Lewis, that the provenance of the books is good and that they are not merely myths. This debate too is ultimately inconclusive and one ends up throwing the dice again. Still, funny as it may seem, the principal reason I decided to trust the accuracy of the Gospels and Acts and even believe them inspired is because they're so badly written and amateurish. As Lewis pointed out, these aren't the same stuff as the Greek myths nor any other kinds. They're first-hand, eye-witness accounts by people who had very little experience writing, who give intense amounts of detail

5. Matt 7:16

6. Matt 25:36

to often unimportant parts and neglect to fully describe the more important parts. Lewis points out that the speech at Paul's trial in Acts is obviously mishandled because Luke got tired of writing it all down— it ran too long. This is a large reason why I don't follow my Evangelical conservative friends when they go beyond inspiration to believing the Bible is without error. For one thing, that is to set up a deductive structure that ultimately falls apart. If you need the Bible to be inerrant in order to believe in Jesus, then what do you need to believe in the Bible? And saying that the Bible says the Bible is inspired is a circle argument and a logical fallacy. No, I find my inspiration in the fact that with all the contrary evidence displayed in flawed documents coming down from our past by unqualified writers doing an uneven quality job, the truth shines through. All these stumble-bums are used by God in spite of their incompetence. These guys weren't clever writers perpetrating a con; they were amateurs falling over themselves to relay the incredible thing they had witnessed.

But I believe, in spite of the long odds of the dice role, despite the fact that everything comes to me in ancient manuscripts that people debate over, because I recognize him. This recognition, this sense of knowing who Jesus is in spite of every contradiction is in Lewis in *The Silver Chair.* I like to call it "Puddleglum's creed." It comes in the scene I mentioned before, when the witch is putting a spell on Puddleglum and the children and the Prince, trying to convince them that Aslan, and all the world above the ground is metaphors and children's games. Puddleglum, at the cost of burning his foot, stomps out the witch's magical fire and then says:

> Suppose this black pit of a kingdom of yours is the only world. Well, it strikes me as a pretty poor one. And that's a funny thing, when you come to think of it. We're just babies making up a game, if you're right. But four babies playing a game can make a play-world which licks your real world hollow. That's why I'm going to stand by the play world. I'm on Aslan's side even if there isn't any Aslan to lead it. I'm going to live as like a Narnian as I can even if there isn't any Narnia. So, thanking you kindly for our supper, if these two gentlemen and the young lady

> are ready, we're leaving your court at once and setting out in the dark to spend our lives looking for Overland. Not that our lives will be very long, I should think; but that's a small loss if the world's as dull a place as you say.[7]

I don't think I've dreamed up Aslan or his reality in Jesus Christ. I just recognize him. The world clicks and comes together with him and nothing makes sense without him. Puddleglum and I will spend our lives looking for him. I recommend it.

There are much worse things to do with your life, believe me.

7. Lewis, *The Silver Chair*, 155-6.

Sixteen: *Adelante*

> So our lives glide on: the river ends we don't know where, and the sea begins, and then there is no more jumping ashore.
>
> —*Felix Holt, the Radical*, George Eliot

If I can sum it all up, you don't have to be any particular political stripe to consider the carpenter from Nazareth. And look at him yourself. Don't rely on people to interpret him for you. The thing I'd most point out is that given the politics of his day of the Sadducees (liberals) who advocated living like Greeks and Romans and not worrying about being so Jewish, and the Pharisees (conservatives) who had the Jewish law and life codified down to every persnickety little thing, *Jesus did not take a side*. "You have heard that it was said, 'Love your neighbor and hate your enemy.' But I tell you love your enemies and pray for those who persecute you."[1] Notice that he rather rises above the fight over what should be the rules and tells his followers to step out into a love so radical and so far above ticking off rules, that you love the people who are trying to kill you. Jesus doesn't go right or left; he goes above and beyond.

And that's what's missing when people try to pretend their political systems and philosophies are "Christian." You may recall that this is "Christianity and," that is when one tries to glue Christianity to their philosophy. And, as Lewis pointed out, the inevitable result is people doing horrible things for their cause and pretending God told them to do it. Christianity always suffers

1. Matt 5:43,44

when people try to hijack it for their politics or their cause. In the end, Christ is infinitely above our human philosophies and systemizations. On one hand there have always been people proposing radical utopias and claiming to do it in Christ's name. They fail. And there have always been people who have equated traditional values with Christian values and predicted that the world was going to Hell because it was changing, that change was evil, and that Christ would come soon and put a stop to all this change. You hear that line a lot now from the Christian right. But it's not original; it was used as justification to cut off the head of King Charles I in 1649. It's an old refrain that has been sung a lot over the centuries. Still, things do change, and often for the better. Change is never inherently evil nor good. But all this is just the dust of history. The point again is: Jesus doesn't go right or left; he goes above and beyond. If you feel drawn to him, that's where you will find him.

As for me, now, my daughter is grown and married and I'm months away from retiring from high school teaching in the *barrio* after 33 years. That's the bright side. My painting has become more and more important. I hope to make a second career of it in retirement, partly to honor my father's memory. My writing is thriving too. I published two scholarly books and a revised version of my novel *The Sun is But a Morning Star*. I continue to edit and publish poetry. My music has gone in a folky direction and after retirement I may start playing coffee houses like I did when I was young.

There is always a dark side. I am sorry to report, however, but in these years, I'm surrounded with death: first my father in 2004, my best friend Bob in 2014 to cancer, to my mother in 2016. I have had my fill of burying people and executing their wills. Even my beloved Golden Retriever, Lizzy, (named after the hero of *Pride and Prejudice*) slipped away two months after Bob. And most recently, my sister in law, Linda, again to that devil, cancer.

Enough already! Just stop!

People have said that your older years are the best years of your life. I have not found it so. Sure, I'd want to keep the wisdom, but the declining energy and ability frankly sucks. And death is as bad as people make it out to be, or worse. Yet, there is new life too, new nieces and nephews being born in the family. Joy and death seem to circle endlessly in this life. That is the dance of humanity. I have found my road and am walking the last long stretch of it.

It helped me to have guides: Bruce Thielemann and Jack Lewis I've already mentioned. Two other writers that are also people of faith have given me much: first, the Presbyterian minister and novelist, Frederick Buechner is a profound guide, and fun to read. Start with *Godric*. Second, the novelist Madeleine L'Engle, famous for *A Wrinkle in Time*, but whose other work is filled with grace and wisdom, has been a guide to me. Read anything by these two and you'll not regret it. Also, if you want to get a good grasp on Lewis and not have to read everything before you do, a good place to start is my friend, Paul Ford's anthology of profound Lewis quotes organized by issue and theme, *Words to Live By: A Guide for the Merely Christian*. It's a wonderful anteroom from where you can branch off in different directions deeper into Lewis' writing and thought with some idea of where you're going.

I don't love death—to be quite honest I really, really hate it, and cancer and strokes. Devil take them all! But I believe the Christ waits for me on the other side. Don't get me wrong, unless there's something I don't know about coming my way, I'll be around for a while yet. But something I would never had understood when I was young stares me in the face now. The clock is running. I find myself focusing on things I want to do before I go. When you're 20-something you feel like you'll live forever. When you're 60-something you know better.

Still, I want to meet Him face to face, as Bob has now done. There is something to that. I won't love it, but I won't fear it either. Mom and Dad and Bob await me there. Who knows, maybe even Lizzy will be there wagging her tail. As they say in Spanish, *¡adelante!*

Bibliography

Lewis, C.S. *An Experiment in Criticism*. Cambridge: Cambridge University Press, 1961.
———. *The Last Battle*. New York: Macmillan, 1988.
———. *Letters to Malcolm, Chiefly on Prayer.* San Diego: Harcourt, 1964.
———. *Mere Christianity*. New York: Collier, 1943.
———. *On Stories and Other Essays on Literature*. San Diego: Harcourt, 1962.
———. *Reflections on the Psalms*. San Diego: Harcourt, 1958.
———. *Selected Literary Essays.*Cambridge: Cambridge University Press, 1969.
———. *The Silver Chair.* New York: Macmillan, 1988.
———. *Surprised by Joy.* San Diego: Harcourt, 1955.
Prothero, James and Donald T. Williams. *Gaining a Face: the Romanticism of C.S. Lewis*. Newcastle: Cambridge Scholars, 2013.

www.ingramcontent.com/pod-product-compliance
Lightning Source LLC
Chambersburg PA
CBHW071059090426
42737CB00013B/2387
9781532618536